# MASTERING JAVASCRIPT ES6

The Next-Gen JavaScript Syntax Explained

THOMPSON CARTER

## Table of Contents

# INTRODUCTION

## *Mastering JavaScript ES6: The Next-Gen JavaScript Syntax Explained*

JavaScript has come a long way since its humble beginnings as a scripting language for web browsers. It has evolved into a versatile, powerful, and indispensable tool for modern developers, underpinning everything from dynamic websites to full-stack applications and even serverless architectures. At the heart of this transformation is ECMAScript 2015, more commonly known as ES6, which revolutionized the way we write and think about JavaScript.

In this book, ***Mastering JavaScript ES6: The Next-Gen JavaScript Syntax Explained***, we will take a deep dive into the features and concepts introduced with ES6, focusing on how they simplify code, promote better practices, and align JavaScript with the needs of modern development. This is not just a guide to syntax; it is a roadmap to mastering a paradigm shift in JavaScript programming, with real-world examples and practical applications at every step.

### *Why ES6 Is a Game-Changer*

Before ES6, JavaScript had its quirks—limitations that often required developers to adopt convoluted workarounds. With ES6, JavaScript entered a new era, introducing a suite of tools and features that brought clarity, efficiency, and scalability to the language. Features such as block-scoped variables (let and const), arrow functions, and template literals allow developers to write cleaner, more concise code. Meanwhile, concepts like Promises and async/await revolutionized asynchronous programming, making it more intuitive and less error-prone.

For developers who want to stay relevant and competitive, understanding ES6 is non-negotiable. It forms the backbone of modern JavaScript frameworks, libraries, and tools. Whether you are building single-page applications with React, managing state with Redux, or creating backend services with Node.js, the principles of ES6 are foundational.

***What You Will Learn***

This book is structured into 20 carefully curated chapters, each designed to explore a key aspect of ES6 in depth. Here's a glimpse of what lies ahead:

- **Chapter 1:** We start with an overview of ES6 and its significance in modern development. You'll set up your environment and get a clear picture of what's to come.
- **Core Syntax Updates:** From block-scoped variables (let and const) to concise and expressive arrow functions, early chapters will redefine how you think about JavaScript fundamentals.

- **Strings and Objects:** Dive into template literals for dynamic string manipulation and enhanced object literals for more efficient object creation.
- **Destructuring and Operators:** Learn how destructuring assignments and the spread/rest operators unlock new levels of flexibility and readability.
- **Advanced Concepts:** As we progress, we'll unravel classes, modules, and the intricacies of Promises and asynchronous programming.
- **Data Structures and Beyond:** Discover how ES6 redefines data handling with Map, Set, symbols, and iterables, offering new tools to solve old problems.
- **Applied Learning:** Culminate your journey with practical applications, exploring how ES6 features integrate seamlessly into real-world projects.

### *Who Is This Book For?*

This book is for anyone who wants to master JavaScript development. Whether you're a beginner with a basic understanding of JavaScript or an experienced developer looking to upgrade your skills, ***Mastering JavaScript ES6*** is tailored to meet you where you are.

- **Beginners** will appreciate the jargon-free explanations and hands-on examples that demystify advanced concepts.

- **Intermediate developers** will gain a deeper understanding of ES6 features and learn best practices to write robust, maintainable code.
- **Experienced developers** will find fresh insights into optimizing workflows and leveraging ES6 to its fullest potential.

### *Why Jargon-Free Matters*

JavaScript documentation and tutorials often suffer from an overload of technical jargon, making learning unnecessarily difficult. In this book, we break down concepts into simple, digestible explanations, always grounded in real-world scenarios. This isn't about memorizing syntax—it's about understanding how to wield ES6 effectively in your everyday work.

### *Real-World Examples at Every Step*

Theory alone won't make you a master developer. Each chapter includes practical examples and exercises that show how ES6 is applied in professional environments. From refactoring legacy code to writing cleaner, more scalable new code, you'll see exactly how ES6 can transform your development process.

### *Looking Ahead*

While ES6 marked a turning point, JavaScript has continued to evolve with subsequent versions. The final chapter of this book will look beyond ES6, giving you a glimpse of newer features and trends to keep you prepared for the future of JavaScript development.

By the time you finish this book, you won't just understand ES6—you'll have the confidence to integrate its features into your projects, streamline your codebase, and embrace a more modern, elegant style of programming. Welcome to the world of next-generation JavaScript. Let's begin the journey.

# CHAPTER 1: INTRODUCTION TO ES6

JavaScript has grown far beyond its original purpose as a scripting language for simple web interactions. Today, it is a cornerstone of web development, powering everything from interactive user interfaces to server-side applications. This chapter explores the evolution of JavaScript, the significance of ES6 in modern development, and how to set up your environment to get started with this groundbreaking update.

## *The Evolution of JavaScript*

JavaScript was introduced in 1995 as a lightweight scripting language designed to bring interactivity to static HTML pages. Its early versions were rudimentary, with limited features and inconsistent implementation across browsers. Despite its simplicity, JavaScript quickly gained popularity due to its ability to create dynamic, responsive web pages.

Key milestones in JavaScript's journey include:

- **1997:** ECMAScript, the standardized version of JavaScript, was established, providing a common specification for browser implementations.

- **2009:** The release of ECMAScript 5 (ES5) introduced essential features like strict mode, array methods (map, filter, reduce), and JSON support.
- **2015:** ECMAScript 2015 (ES6) marked a turning point with significant updates that modernized the language. It added features like block-scoped variables, classes, Promises, and modules, aligning JavaScript with the needs of modern development.

Since ES6, JavaScript has continued to evolve with annual updates. However, ES6 remains the foundation for modern JavaScript development, forming the basis for many subsequent features.

### *Why ES6 Matters in Modern Development*

ES6 was a response to the growing demands placed on JavaScript by developers building complex web applications. Prior to ES6, developers had to rely on cumbersome workarounds or third-party libraries to address JavaScript's limitations. ES6 solved many of these challenges by introducing features that made code more concise, readable, and maintainable.

Key benefits of ES6 in modern development include:

- **Improved Readability:** Features like let, const, and template literals make code more expressive and easier to understand.
- **Enhanced Functionality:** New syntax for classes and modules aligns JavaScript with object-oriented programming principles.
- **Asynchronous Programming:** Promises and async/await simplify working with asynchronous operations, a cornerstone of modern web development.
- **Code Modularity:** The introduction of ES6 modules makes it easier to organize and reuse code across projects.
- **Browser Compatibility:** Although not all browsers natively support ES6, tools like Babel allow developers to write ES6 code and transpile it for older environments.

For developers, learning ES6 is not just about adopting new syntax—it's about embracing a modern way of writing JavaScript that is more aligned with current best practices and frameworks.

***Setting Up Your Environment for ES6***

Before you can start using ES6, you'll need to ensure your development environment is configured correctly. Here's a step-by-step guide:

1. **Choose a Code Editor:**

- A good code editor can significantly improve your development experience. Popular choices include:
    - VS Code: Lightweight, extensible, and ideal for JavaScript.
    - Sublime Text or Atom: Alternatives with strong JavaScript support.

2. **Install Node.js and npm:**
    - Node.js allows you to run JavaScript outside the browser, while npm (Node Package Manager) helps you manage packages.
    - Download and install Node.js from the official website. The installer includes npm by default.
    - Verify the installation:

```bash
node -v
npm -v
```

3. **Set Up Babel:**
    - Babel is a JavaScript transpiler that converts ES6 code into ES5, ensuring compatibility with older browsers.
    - To set up Babel:
        - Initialize a project:

```bash
mkdir es6-project
cd es6-project
npm init -y
```

- Install Babel:

```bash
npm install @babel/core @babel/cli @babel/preset-env --save-dev
```

- Configure Babel by creating a .babelrc file:

```json
{
  "presets": ["@babel/preset-env"]
}
```

4. **Set Up a Local Server:**
   - For testing ES6 modules, you need a local server since ES6 modules require a module loader.
   - Use http-server:

   bash

```
npm install -g http-server
http-server
```

5. **Verify Your Setup:**
   - Create a simple index.html file that includes an ES6 script:

```html
<!DOCTYPE html>
<html lang="en">
<head>
  <meta charset="UTF-8">
  <meta name="viewport" content="width=device-width, initial-scale=1.0">
  <title>ES6 Test</title>
</head>
<body>
  <script type="module">
    const greet = () => console.log("Hello, ES6!");
    greet();
  </script>
</body>
</html>
```

- Open this file using your local server to confirm everything works.

Now that you understand the evolution of JavaScript, the importance of ES6, and how to set up your environment, you're ready to dive into the new syntax and features that make ES6 a game-changer. In the next chapter, we'll start by exploring let and const—the foundation of ES6 variable declarations. Let's get started!

# CHAPTER 2: LET AND CONST – THE NEW VARIABLE DECLARATIONS

JavaScript's journey toward better code readability and maintainability took a significant leap forward with the introduction of let and const in ES6. These two keywords addressed long-standing issues with the traditional var declaration, giving developers more control over variable scoping and improving code safety. In this chapter, we'll examine the key differences between var, let, and const, explore scoping rules, and establish best practices for declaring variables.

***Differences Between var, let, and const***

To understand why let and const are essential improvements, let's first review the behavior of var:

1. **var:**
   - **Hoisting**: Variables declared with var are hoisted to the top of their scope but initialized as undefined.

     javascript

     ```
     console.log(x); // undefined
     var x = 5;
     ```

- **Function Scope**: var is scoped to the nearest function, ignoring block scope.

  javascript

  ```
  if (true) {
    var y = 10;
  }
  console.log(y); // 10
  ```

- **Redeclaration**: Variables can be redeclared within the same scope.

  javascript

  ```
  var z = 1;
  var z = 2; // No error
  ```

2. **let:**

   - **No Hoisting (Temporal Dead Zone)**: Variables declared with let are not accessible before their declaration.

     javascript

     ```
     console.log(a); // ReferenceError
     let a = 5;
     ```

- **Block Scope**: let is scoped to the block in which it is declared.

  javascript

  ```
  if (true) {
    let b = 10;
  }
  console.log(b); // ReferenceError
  ```

- **No Redeclaration**: Redeclaring a variable in the same scope results in an error.

  javascript

  ```
  let c = 1;
  let c = 2; // SyntaxError
  ```

3. **const:**

   - **Constant Value**: const is used to declare variables whose value will not be reassigned.

     javascript

     ```
     const d = 3;
     d = 4; // TypeError
     ```

- **Block Scope**: Like let, const is also block-scoped.
- **Declaration and Initialization**: Variables declared with const must be initialized at the time of declaration.

  javascript

  ```
  const e; // SyntaxError: Missing initializer
  ```

- **Mutable Objects**: While const ensures the reference cannot be changed, the content of the object can be modified.

  javascript

  ```
  const obj = { name: "John" };
  obj.name = "Doe"; // No error
  console.log(obj.name); // "Doe"
  ```

- Use let for variables that will change over time.
- Use const for values that should remain constant, such as configuration settings.

### *Scoping Rules: Block, Function, and Global*

Scoping rules define where variables are accessible within your code. ES6 introduced block-scoped declarations (let and const) to complement the function-scoped var.

1. **Global Scope:**
   - Variables declared outside any block or function are global and accessible throughout the program.
   - Using var, let, or const in the global scope behaves similarly, but avoid var for safety reasons.
2. **Function Scope:**
   - Variables declared within a function are accessible only within that function.
   - var, let, and const follow function-scoping rules:

     ```javascript
     function greet() {
       let name = "Alice";
       console.log(name); // Alice
     }
     console.log(name); // ReferenceError
     ```

3. **Block Scope:**
   - Block scope is introduced with let and const. Variables declared with these keywords are

accessible only within the block {} in which they are defined.

javascript

```
if (true) {
  let x = 20;
  const y = 30;
}
console.log(x); // ReferenceError
console.log(y); // ReferenceError
```

4. **Shadowing:**
   - Variables declared in a nested scope with the same name as a variable in the outer scope shadow the outer variable.

     javascript

     ```
     let z = 10;
     if (true) {
       let z = 20;
       console.log(z); // 20 (inner)
     }
     console.log(z); // 10 (outer)
     ```

5. **Hoisting Behavior:**

- var variables are hoisted and initialized as undefined.
- let and const are hoisted but remain uninitialized (Temporal Dead Zone) until the interpreter reaches their declaration.

```javascript
console.log(a); // undefined
var a = 5;

console.log(b); // ReferenceError
let b = 10;
```

***Best Practices for Variable Declaration***

1. **Prefer const Over let:**
   - Default to const for all variables unless you anticipate reassigning their values. This makes your code more predictable and easier to debug.

```javascript
const config = {
  apiEndpoint: "https://api.example.com",
};
```

2. **Minimize Scope:**
    - Declare variables in the narrowest scope possible to reduce side effects and improve readability.

    javascript

    ```
    function calculateTotal(items) {
      let total = 0;
      for (let i = 0; i < items.length; i++) {
        total += items[i];
      }
      return total;
    }
    ```

3. **Avoid Global Variables:**
    - Global variables can lead to conflicts and unintended behavior. Use const and let to confine variables to specific blocks or functions.
4. **Name Variables Clearly:**
    - Use descriptive names to make your code self-documenting.

    javascript

    ```
    const maxUsers = 100;
    let currentUsers = 0;
    ```

5. **Be Consistent:**
   - Establish team-wide guidelines for when to use let and const. Stick to conventions to ensure code consistency across projects.

Now that you've mastered the differences between var, let, and const, as well as scoping rules and best practices, you're equipped to write safer and more maintainable JavaScript code. In the next chapter, we'll build on this foundation by exploring arrow functions—a key feature of ES6 that simplifies how we write functions. Let's continue!

# CHAPTER 3: ARROW FUNCTIONS – SIMPLIFYING SYNTAX

The introduction of arrow functions in ES6 revolutionized how JavaScript developers write functions. With a more concise syntax, arrow functions reduce boilerplate while addressing some long-standing quirks of traditional function expressions. However, with their advantages come new considerations, especially when dealing with scoping and practical use cases.

In this chapter, we will explore the syntax of arrow functions, delve into their unique behavior regarding lexical scoping of this, and highlight practical applications as well as common pitfalls.

### *Understanding Arrow Function Syntax*

Arrow functions offer a shorter syntax for defining functions. Here's how they differ from traditional function expressions:

1. **Basic Syntax:**
   - A typical function:

     javascript

     ```
     function add(a, b) {
       return a + b;
     ```

```
}
```

- With an arrow function:

  javascript

  ```
  const add = (a, b) => a + b;
  ```

2. **Key Features:**
   - **Omission of function keyword:** Arrow functions eliminate the need for the function keyword.
   - **Implicit return:** If the function body consists of a single expression, it can return the result implicitly without using the return keyword.

     javascript

     ```
     const square = x => x * x; // Implicit return
     ```

   - **Parentheses around parameters:**
     - Single parameter: Parentheses are optional.

       javascript

       ```
       const double = x => x * 2;
       ```

- No parameters or multiple parameters: Parentheses are mandatory.

```javascript
const sayHello = () => "Hello!";
const multiply = (x, y) => x * y;
```

3. **Block Body Syntax:**
   - For functions requiring multiple lines or statements, use curly braces {} and explicitly include the return statement:

```javascript
const calculate = (a, b) => {
  const result = a * b + 10;
  return result;
};
```

### *Lexical Scoping of this*

One of the most impactful changes with arrow functions is their handling of this. Unlike traditional functions, arrow functions do not have their own this. Instead, they lexically inherit this from the surrounding context.

1. **Traditional Functions:**
    - In traditional functions, this depends on how the function is called.

    javascript

    ```
    function Traditional() {
      console.log(this); // Value depends on call site
    }
    ```

2. **Arrow Functions:**
    - Arrow functions bind this to the context in which they were defined, not the context in which they are executed.

    javascript

    ```
    const ArrowExample = {
      name: "Arrow",
      printThis: () => console.log(this), // Inherits `this` from the surrounding scope
    };
    ArrowExample.printThis(); // Usually undefined or window in browsers
    ```

3. **Practical Use in Callbacks:**

- Arrow functions shine in scenarios where maintaining this is essential, such as event handlers or callbacks.

javascript

```
function Timer() {
  this.seconds = 0;
  setInterval(() => {
    this.seconds++;
    console.log(this.seconds);
  }, 1000);
}
new Timer(); // Correctly increments `this.seconds`
```

- In comparison, a traditional function would lose the context of this unless explicitly bound:

javascript

```
function Timer() {
  this.seconds = 0;
  setInterval(function () {
    this.seconds++; // `this` is undefined or window
    console.log(this.seconds);
  }.bind(this), 1000);
```

```
}
new Timer();
```

4. **No arguments Object:**
   - Arrow functions do not have their own arguments object. To access arguments, use rest parameters:

     javascript

     ```
     const add = (...args) => args.reduce((a, b) => a + b, 0);
     console.log(add(1, 2, 3)); // 6
     ```

***Practical Examples and Common Pitfalls***

Arrow functions are powerful, but they require careful use. Let's explore practical examples and potential challenges.

1. **Practical Examples:**
   - **Event Listeners:**

     javascript

     ```
     document.querySelector("#button").addEventListener("click", () => {
       console.log("Button clicked!");
     });
     ```

- **Array Methods:**

  javascript

  ```
  const numbers = [1, 2, 3];
  const squares = numbers.map(x => x * x);
  console.log(squares); // [1, 4, 9]
  ```

- **Object Methods (with caution):**
  - Arrow functions are not suitable for defining methods in objects, as they lack their own this:

    javascript

    ```
    const obj = {
     value: 42,
     method: () => console.log(this.value), //
    Incorrect: `this` is inherited
    };
    obj.method(); // Undefined or unexpected
    value
    ```

2. **Common Pitfalls:**
   - **Using Arrow Functions as Constructors:**
     - Arrow functions cannot be used as constructors because they lack their own this:

javascript

```
const Person = (name) => {
 this.name = name; // Error: `this` is
undefined
};
const john = new Person("John"); //
TypeError
```

- **Context Sensitivity:**
  - Since arrow functions inherit this from the surrounding context, they may not behave as expected when nested:

    javascript

    ```
    const obj = {
     value: 10,
     nested: () => {
      console.log(this.value); // Undefined or
    unexpected
     },
    };
    obj.nested();
    ```

- **Misuse in Object Methods:**

- Use regular functions for methods that require their own this:

```javascript
const obj = {
  value: 42,
  method() {
    console.log(this.value); // Correct: 42
  },
};
obj.method();
```

### *Best Practices for Arrow Functions*

- Use arrow functions for short, concise callbacks and functions where this context should be inherited.
- Avoid arrow functions for object methods or scenarios requiring their own this.
- Remember that arrow functions are not suitable as constructors.

Arrow functions are just one piece of the ES6 puzzle. Now that you've mastered their syntax, behavior, and best practices, it's time to explore another powerful feature: template literals. In the next chapter, we'll dive into this feature and see how it transforms string manipulation in JavaScript. Let's continue!

# CHAPTER 4: TEMPLATE LITERALS – STRING INTERPOLATION MADE EASY

Strings are one of the most fundamental components of any programming language, and JavaScript is no exception. Before ES6, working with strings often involved clunky concatenation using the + operator, especially when variables or expressions needed to be embedded. With the introduction of template literals in ES6, string manipulation has become significantly more powerful, expressive, and easier to work with.

In this chapter, we'll explore how to create dynamic strings using template literals, leverage multiline strings and embedded expressions, and tap into the power of tagged templates for advanced use cases.

### *Creating Dynamic Strings with Template Literals*

Template literals are a new way of handling strings in JavaScript. They are defined using backticks (`) instead of single or double quotes and provide enhanced flexibility.

1. **Basic Syntax:**
    - A string enclosed in backticks:

```javascript
const simpleString = `Hello, World!`;
console.log(simpleString); // "Hello, World!"
```

2. **String Interpolation:**
   - Template literals support placeholders for variables and expressions, enclosed in ${}.

```javascript
const name = "John";
const age = 30;
const message = `My name is ${name} and I am ${age} years old.`;
console.log(message); // "My name is John and I am 30 years old."
```

3. **Expressions Inside Placeholders:**
   - You can include any valid JavaScript expression within the placeholders.

```javascript
const a = 5;
const b = 10;
```

```
console.log(`The sum of ${a} and ${b} is ${a + b}.`); // "The sum of 5 and 10 is 15."
```

4. **Advantages Over Concatenation:**
   - Simplifies code readability and avoids errors caused by mismatched quotes or concatenation symbols.

     javascript

     ```
     // Before ES6
     const oldWay = "Hello, " + name + "! You are " + age + " years old.";
     // With Template Literals
     const newWay = `Hello, ${name}! You are ${age} years old.`;
     ```

***Multiline Strings and Embedded Expressions***

Template literals make working with multiline strings and complex expressions more elegant.

1. **Multiline Strings:**
   - Before ES6, creating multiline strings required cumbersome workarounds using newline characters (\n) or concatenation.

     javascript

```
// Before ES6
const oldMultiline = "This is line one.\n" + "This is line two.";
console.log(oldMultiline);

// With Template Literals
const newMultiline = `This is line one.
This is line two.`;
console.log(newMultiline);
```

2. **Preserving Whitespace:**
   - Template literals retain formatting, including spaces and line breaks.

javascript

```
const poem = `
  Roses are red,
  Violets are blue,
  Template literals are awesome,
  And so are you.
`;
console.log(poem);
```

3. **Combining Multiline and Embedded Expressions:**

- You can seamlessly mix multiline strings with interpolated variables or expressions.

javascript

```
const item = "laptop";
const price = 1200;
const multilineMessage = `
  Order Details:
  ----------------
  Item: ${item}
  Price: $${price}
  Tax (10%): $${(price * 0.1).toFixed(2)}
  Total: $${(price * 1.1).toFixed(2)}
`;
console.log(multilineMessage);
```

***Using Tagged Templates for Advanced Applications***

Tagged templates provide a way to customize how template literals are processed. By defining a function (a tag), you can manipulate the output of the template literal.

1. **Basic Tagged Template Syntax:**
   - A tagged template uses a function to process the literal and placeholders.

```javascript
function tag(strings, ...values) {
  console.log(strings); // Array of string segments
  console.log(values); // Array of interpolated values
}
tag`Hello, ${name}. You are ${age} years old.`;
```

2. **Applications of Tagged Templates:**
   - **Escaping Special Characters:**
     - Prevent potential security issues, such as SQL injection or XSS.

```javascript
function escapeHTML(strings, ...values) {
  return strings.reduce((result, str, i) => {
    const escape = str => str.replace(/</g, "&lt;").replace(/>/g, "&gt;");
    return result + str + (values[i] !== undefined ? escape(values[i]) : "");
  }, "");
}
const userInput = "<script>alert('Hack!')</script>";
```

```
console.log(escapeHTML`User input:
${userInput}`);
```

- **Custom Formatting:**
  - Format numbers, dates, or currencies dynamically.

javascript

```
function currency(strings, ...values) {
  return strings.reduce((result, str, i) => {
    const formatted = values[i] !== undefined
? `$${values[i].toFixed(2)}` : "";
    return result + str + formatted;
  }, "");
}
const price = 19.99;
console.log(currency`The total is:
${price}`);
```

- **Localization:**
  - Translate strings dynamically based on locale settings.

javascript

```
const translations = {
```

```
  en: { hello: "Hello" },
  es: { hello: "Hola" },
};
function localize(strings, ...values) {
  const lang = "es";
  return strings.reduce(
    (result, str, i) => result + (translations[lang][str.trim()] || str) + (values[i] || ""),
    ""
  );
}
console.log(localize`hello, world`);
```

3. **Performance Considerations:**
   - Use tagged templates judiciously for scenarios where customization justifies the added complexity.
   - Benchmark tagged templates if performance is critical, especially in large-scale applications.

### *Best Practices for Template Literals*

- Use template literals for cleaner and more readable string interpolation.

- Leverage multiline capabilities for improved formatting of logs, emails, or UI templates.
- Employ tagged templates for advanced processing, such as escaping or localization, but keep them modular and well-documented.

Template literals make string manipulation simpler and more expressive. Now that you've mastered their syntax and capabilities, the next chapter will focus on **destructuring assignment**, a powerful feature that simplifies the process of unpacking values from arrays and objects. Let's dive in!

# CHAPTER 5: DESTRUCTURING ASSIGNMENT

Destructuring assignment is one of the most powerful and elegant features introduced in ES6. It simplifies the process of extracting values from arrays or objects and assigning them to variables. Whether you're handling API responses, manipulating data structures, or refactoring code for clarity, destructuring helps reduce boilerplate and improves readability.

In this chapter, we'll cover the basics of array and object destructuring, explore nested destructuring and default values, and examine real-world use cases in APIs and frameworks.

### *Array and Object Destructuring*

1. **Array Destructuring:**
   - Extract values from arrays and assign them to variables in a single line:

     javascript

     ```
     const fruits = ["apple", "banana", "cherry"];
     ```

```
const [first, second, third] = fruits;
console.log(first); // "apple"
console.log(second); // "banana"
console.log(third); // "cherry"
```

- **Skipping Elements:**
  - Use commas to skip unwanted values:

    javascript

    ```
    const numbers = [1, 2, 3, 4];
    const [first, , third] = numbers;
    console.log(first); // 1
    console.log(third); // 3
    ```

- **Rest Operator:**
  - Capture the remaining elements of an array:

    javascript

    ```
    const colors = ["red", "green", "blue", "yellow"];
    const [primary, secondary, ...others] = colors;
    console.log(primary); // "red"
    console.log(others); // ["blue", "yellow"]
    ```

2. **Object Destructuring:**
   - Extract values from objects by matching keys:

     javascript

     ```
     const person = { name: "John", age: 30, profession:
     "Developer" };
     const { name, age } = person;
     console.log(name); // "John"
     console.log(age); // 30
     ```

   - **Renaming Variables:**
     - Assign values to variables with different names:

       javascript

       ```
       const user = { id: 42, username: "johndoe"
       };
       const { id: userId, username: userName } =
       user;
       console.log(userId); // 42
       console.log(userName); // "johndoe"
       ```

   - **Rest Properties:**
     - Extract remaining properties into a new object:

javascript

```
const book = { title: "ES6 Guide", author: "Jane Doe", year: 2023 };
const { title, ...details } = book;
console.log(title); // "ES6 Guide"
console.log(details); // { author: "Jane Doe", year: 2023 }
```

### *Nested Destructuring and Default Values*

1. **Nested Destructuring:**
   - Extract values from deeply nested arrays or objects:

     javascript

     ```
     const data = { user: { name: "Alice", info: { age: 25, city: "NYC" } } };
     const {
       user: {
         name,
         info: { age, city },
       },
     } = data;
     console.log(name); // "Alice"
     ```

```
console.log(age); // 25
console.log(city); // "NYC"
```

- For arrays:

javascript

```
const matrix = [[1, 2], [3, 4]];
const [[a, b], [c, d]] = matrix;
console.log(a, b, c, d); // 1 2 3 4
```

2. **Default Values:**
   - Provide default values for variables if the array or object doesn't contain the key or value:

javascript

```
const user = { name: "Bob" };
const { name, age = 18 } = user;
console.log(name); // "Bob"
console.log(age); // 18
```

- Works with arrays too:

javascript

```
const numbers = [1];
```

```
const [x, y = 2] = numbers;
console.log(x); // 1
console.log(y); // 2
```

### *Real-World Use Cases in APIs and Frameworks*

1. **Working with API Responses:**
   - APIs often return structured data in JSON format. Destructuring makes it easy to extract relevant information.

     javascript

     ```
     const apiResponse = {
       data: {
         id: 101,
         name: "Product A",
         price: 50,
         stock: { available: 120, reserved: 10 },
       },
     };

     const {
       data: {
         name,
     ```

```
    price,
    stock: { available },
  },
} = apiResponse;

console.log(name); // "Product A"
console.log(price); // 50
console.log(available); // 120
```

2. **Handling Function Parameters:**
   - Use destructuring in function arguments for cleaner code:

     javascript

     ```
     const printUser = ({ name, age }) => {
       console.log(`Name: ${name}, Age: ${age}`);
     };

     const user = { name: "Alice", age: 25, location: "London" };
     printUser(user);
     ```

3. **State Management in Frameworks:**
   - Destructuring is extensively used in frameworks like React for managing state and props.

```javascript
const [state, setState] = useState(0);
console.log(state); // Current state
setState(1); // Update state
```

4. **Processing Dynamic Data:**
   - Destructuring simplifies operations on dynamically generated or fetched data:

```javascript
const data = [
  { id: 1, value: "A" },
  { id: 2, value: "B" },
];

data.forEach(({ id, value }) => {
  console.log(`ID: ${id}, Value: ${value}`);
});
```

### *Best Practices for Destructuring*

1. **Start Simple:**

   - Use basic destructuring for small, manageable data structures. Avoid over-complicating destructuring with deeply nested objects unless necessary.
2. **Combine with Defaults:**
   - Always provide default values for optional properties to prevent runtime errors.
3. **Use Aliases for Clarity:**
   - Rename variables when destructuring to avoid name conflicts or improve readability.
4. **Keep Functions Clean:**
   - Leverage destructuring in function parameters for simpler and more descriptive function signatures.

Destructuring is a powerful feature that simplifies handling complex data structures, particularly in modern applications where JSON and APIs dominate. Armed with this knowledge, you're ready to explore the **spread and rest operators** in the next chapter, which provide further tools for flexible and expressive JavaScript programming. Let's continue!

# CHAPTER 6: ENHANCED OBJECT LITERALS

Enhanced object literals in ES6 introduce a more concise and expressive way to define objects. These enhancements reduce boilerplate, improve readability, and enable dynamic property creation, making objects more versatile in modern JavaScript development.

In this chapter, we'll explore the new syntax for defining properties and methods, delve into computed property names for dynamic keys, and discuss how enhanced object literals can be applied in data modeling.

## *Shortened Syntax for Properties and Methods*

1. **Property Value Shorthand:**
   - Prior to ES6, when defining an object, you had to explicitly map variable names to object properties, even if they shared the same name:

     javascript

```
const name = "Alice";
const age = 25;

// Before ES6
const user = {
  name: name,
  age: age,
};

console.log(user); // { name: "Alice", age: 25 }
```

- With ES6, if the variable name matches the property name, you can use a shorthand:

  javascript

  ```
  const user = { name, age };
  console.log(user); // { name: "Alice", age: 25 }
  ```

2. **Method Shorthand:**
   - Defining methods within objects is more concise with ES6:

     javascript

     ```
     // Before ES6
     ```

```
const user = {
  greet: function () {
    console.log("Hello!");
  },
};

// With ES6
const user = {
  greet() {
    console.log("Hello!");
  },
};

user.greet(); // "Hello!"
```

- This shorthand syntax is especially useful in frameworks where methods are defined frequently, such as React or Vue.

***Computed Property Names***

ES6 allows the use of expressions within square brackets ([]) to define property names dynamically, making objects more flexible and capable of modeling complex scenarios.

1. **Dynamic Keys:**

- With computed property names, you can generate object keys at runtime:

```javascript
const key = "status";
const value = "active";

const user = {
  id: 1,
  [key]: value,
};

console.log(user); // { id: 1, status: "active" }
```

2. **Combining Static and Computed Properties:**
   - Objects can mix static keys and computed keys seamlessly:

```javascript
const baseKey = "level";
const settings = {
  mode: "dark",
  [baseKey + 1]: "beginner",
  [baseKey + 2]: "advanced",
```

```
};

console.log(settings); // { mode: "dark", level1: "beginner", level2: "advanced" }
```

3. **Applications in Loops:**
   - Computed property names are particularly useful when creating objects programmatically:

```javascript
const keys = ["firstName", "lastName", "age"];
const values = ["John", "Doe", 30];

const user = {};
keys.forEach((key, index) => {
  user[key] = values[index];
});

console.log(user); // { firstName: "John", lastName: "Doe", age: 30 }
```

***Using Enhanced Object Literals in Data Modeling***

1. **Creating Data Structures:**

- Enhanced object literals simplify the process of defining and initializing data structures:

javascript

```
const createUser = (id, name, age) => ({
  id,
  name,
  age,
  isActive: true,
});

const user = createUser(1, "Alice", 25);
console.log(user); // { id: 1, name: "Alice", age: 25,
isActive: true }
```

2. **Defining Configurations:**
   - Easily build configuration objects with dynamic keys:

javascript

```
const env = "production";
const config = {
  appName: "MyApp",
```

```
[env === "production" ? "databaseUrl" : "mockDatabase"]: "http://example.com",
};

console.log(config); // { appName: "MyApp", databaseUrl: "http://example.com" }
```

3. **Event Handling in UI Frameworks:**
   - Enhanced object literals are often used in frameworks like React to map dynamic event handlers:

```javascript
const eventHandlers = {
  onClick() {
    console.log("Button clicked!");
  },
  ["on" + "Hover"]() {
    console.log("Button hovered!");
  },
};

eventHandlers.onClick(); // "Button clicked!"
eventHandlers.onHover(); // "Button hovered!"
```

4. **State Management:**
    - Enhanced object literals simplify state updates in applications:

      javascript

      ```
      const updateState = (state, key, value) => ({
        ...state,
        [key]: value,
      });

      const initialState = { count: 0 };
      const newState = updateState(initialState, "count", 1);

      console.log(newState); // { count: 1 }
      ```

### *Best Practices for Enhanced Object Literals*

1. **Use Property Shorthand for Readability:**
    - If variables and properties share the same name, use the shorthand syntax to reduce boilerplate.
2. **Keep Computed Keys Simple:**
    - Avoid overly complex expressions for computed property names to maintain readability.

3. **Combine Shorthand with Default Values:**
   - Use destructuring and shorthand together for clean initialization:

     javascript

     ```
     const initUser = ({ name = "Anonymous", age = 0 }) => ({
       name,
       age,
       active: true,
     });

     console.log(initUser({ age: 25 })); // { name: "Anonymous", age: 25, active: true }
     ```

4. **Embrace Methods in Objects:**
   - Use the method shorthand to make your codebase consistent and modern.

Enhanced object literals streamline object creation and management, making them a vital tool for modern JavaScript development. Armed with these techniques, you're ready to explore the **spread and rest operators** in the next chapter, which further enhance JavaScript's expressiveness and flexibility. Let's continue!

# CHAPTER 7: THE SPREAD AND REST OPERATORS

The spread (...) and rest (...) operators are among the most versatile tools introduced in ES6, transforming how arrays, objects, and function arguments are handled. Despite sharing the same syntax, these operators serve distinct purposes. The spread operator expands data structures into individual elements, while the rest operator collects multiple elements into a single structure.

In this chapter, we'll explore how to expand arrays and objects using the spread operator, collect arguments with the rest operator, and combine these features to write flexible, clean, and expressive JavaScript code.

***Expanding Arrays and Objects with the Spread Operator***

The spread operator (...) allows you to unpack the elements of an array or object into a new structure. This feature is invaluable for creating copies, combining data, or passing values into functions.

1. **Expanding Arrays:**
   - Spread syntax unpacks elements from an array:

     javascript

     ```
     const numbers = [1, 2, 3];
     const expanded = [...numbers, 4, 5];
     console.log(expanded); // [1, 2, 3, 4, 5]
     ```

   - **Copying Arrays:**
     - Create a shallow copy of an array without affecting the original:

       javascript

       ```
       const original = [10, 20, 30];
       const copy = [...original];
       copy[0] = 99;
       console.log(original); // [10, 20, 30]
       console.log(copy); // [99, 20, 30]
       ```

   - **Merging Arrays:**
     - Combine multiple arrays into one:

javascript

```
const arr1 = [1, 2];
const arr2 = [3, 4];
const merged = [...arr1, ...arr2];
console.log(merged); // [1, 2, 3, 4]
```

2. **Expanding Objects:**
   - Spread syntax works similarly with objects, unpacking properties into a new object:

     javascript

     ```
     const user = { name: "Alice", age: 25 };
     const updatedUser = { ...user, age: 26, city: "NYC"
     };
     console.log(updatedUser); // { name: "Alice", age:
     26, city: "NYC" }
     ```

   - **Copying Objects:**
     - Create a shallow copy of an object:

       javascript

       ```
       const original = { key: "value" };
       const copy = { ...original };
       console.log(copy); // { key: "value" }
       ```

- **Merging Objects:**
  - Combine properties from multiple objects:

    ```javascript
    const obj1 = { a: 1, b: 2 };
    const obj2 = { b: 3, c: 4 };
    const merged = { ...obj1, ...obj2 };
    console.log(merged); // { a: 1, b: 3, c: 4 }
    ```

***Collecting Arguments with the Rest Operator***

The rest operator (...) collects multiple elements into an array or object. It is often used in function arguments, array manipulation, and destructuring.

1. **Function Arguments:**
   - Collect all remaining arguments into an array:

     ```javascript
     function sum(...numbers) {
      return numbers.reduce((total, num) => total + num, 0);
     }
     console.log(sum(1, 2, 3, 4)); // 10
     ```

2. **Destructuring Arrays:**
   - Extract specific elements and group the rest into an array:

     javascript

     ```
     const [first, second, ...rest] = [1, 2, 3, 4, 5];
     console.log(first); // 1
     console.log(second); // 2
     console.log(rest); // [3, 4, 5]
     ```

3. **Destructuring Objects:**
   - Separate specific properties and collect the rest:

     javascript

     ```
     const user = { name: "Alice", age: 25, city: "NYC"
     };
     const { name, ...details } = user;
     console.log(name); // "Alice"
     console.log(details); // { age: 25, city: "NYC" }
     ```

***Combining Spread and Rest for Flexible Code***

The power of these operators lies in their ability to simplify complex operations and make code more modular.

1. **Function Defaults with Spread:**
   - Pass array elements as individual arguments to a function:

     javascript

     ```
     const numbers = [1, 2, 3];
     console.log(Math.max(...numbers)); // 3
     ```

2. **Dynamic Property Updates:**
   - Combine spread and rest to update specific properties in objects while keeping others intact:

     javascript

     ```
     const updateUser = (user, updates) => ({ ...user,
     ...updates });
     const user = { name: "Alice", age: 25 };
     const updated = updateUser(user, { age: 26 });
     console.log(updated); // { name: "Alice", age: 26 }
     ```

3. **Filtering Properties:**
   - Use destructuring with rest to exclude specific properties from an object:

     javascript

```javascript
const { password, ...safeUser } = { username: "john", password: "12345", email: "john@example.com" };
console.log(safeUser); // { username: "john", email: "john@example.com" }
```

4. **Combining Arrays and Objects Dynamically:**
   - Merge and manipulate data structures dynamically:

javascript

```javascript
const arr1 = [1, 2];
const arr2 = [3, 4];
const merged = [...arr1, 5, ...arr2];
console.log(merged); // [1, 2, 5, 3, 4]
```

### *Common Pitfalls and Considerations*

1. **Shallow Copies:**
   - Both the spread operator and rest operator create shallow copies. Nested structures remain referenced:

javascript

```javascript
const nested = { a: { b: 1 } };
const copy = { ...nested };
```

```
copy.a.b = 2;
console.log(nested.a.b); // 2
```

2. **Excessive Usage:**
   - While these operators improve readability, overusing them, especially in deeply nested destructuring, can reduce clarity.
3. **Performance:**
   - Copying or merging large arrays or objects using spread may impact performance in resource-intensive applications.

### *Best Practices for Spread and Rest Operators*

1. **Use Spread for Simplicity:**
   - Leverage spread to copy or merge arrays and objects concisely.
2. **Be Cautious with Nested Structures:**
   - For deeply nested objects or arrays, consider using libraries like Lodash for deep cloning.
3. **Keep Rest Parameters Descriptive:**
   - Use meaningful names for rest parameters to improve code clarity:

     javascript

```
function logMessages(firstMessage, ...remainingMessages) {
  console.log(firstMessage);
  console.log(remainingMessages);
}
```

4. **Combine with Other Features:**
   - Pair spread and rest with destructuring for clean and modular code.

The spread and rest operators make JavaScript more expressive, allowing developers to write concise, modular, and flexible code. With these tools mastered, you're ready to explore **classes in ES6**, a major step forward for object-oriented programming in JavaScript. Let's continue!

# CHAPTER 8: CLASSES IN ES6

ES6 introduced classes to JavaScript, providing a clearer and more intuitive syntax for object-oriented programming (OOP). While JavaScript has always supported OOP through prototypes, classes abstract away the complexity, making it easier to write and maintain object-oriented code. In this chapter, we'll explore how ES6 classes work, understand inheritance, learn about static methods and instance properties, and examine practical applications in OOP design patterns.

## *Understanding ES6 Classes and Inheritance*

1. **Defining a Class:**
   - A class is defined using the class keyword. The constructor method initializes class instances.

javascript

```
class Person {
  constructor(name, age) {
    this.name = name;
    this.age = age;
  }

  introduce() {
    console.log(`Hi, I'm ${this.name} and I'm
${this.age} years old.`);
  }
}

const john = new Person("John", 30);
john.introduce(); // "Hi, I'm John and I'm 30 years
old."
```

2. **Class Inheritance:**
   - Use the extends keyword to create subclasses that inherit properties and methods from a parent class.

javascript

```
class Employee extends Person {
  constructor(name, age, jobTitle) {
```

```
  super(name, age); // Calls the parent class constructor
  this.jobTitle = jobTitle;
 }

 work() {
  console.log(`${this.name} is working as a ${this.jobTitle}.`);
 }
}

const alice = new Employee("Alice", 25, "Software Engineer");
alice.introduce(); // "Hi, I'm Alice and I'm 25 years old."
alice.work(); // "Alice is working as a Software Engineer."
```

3. **Overriding Methods:**
   - Subclasses can override methods from the parent class:

javascript

```
class Animal {
 speak() {
```

```
    console.log("Animal speaks.");
  }
}

class Dog extends Animal {
  speak() {
    console.log("Dog barks.");
  }
}

const dog = new Dog();
dog.speak(); // "Dog barks."
```

4. **Key Features of ES6 Classes:**
   - Classes are syntactic sugar over JavaScript's prototype-based inheritance.
   - Methods defined in a class are automatically added to its prototype.
   - Classes are not hoisted; you must define them before using them.

***Static Methods and Instance Properties***

1. **Static Methods:**

- Static methods are defined using the static keyword and belong to the class itself, not the instances.

  javascript

  ```
  class MathUtils {
    static add(a, b) {
      return a + b;
    }
  }

  console.log(MathUtils.add(5, 3)); // 8
  ```

- Use static methods for utility functions that don't depend on instance-specific data.

2. **Instance Properties:**
   - Instance properties are defined inside the constructor method and are unique to each instance:

     javascript

     ```
     class User {
       constructor(username, email) {
         this.username = username;
         this.email = email;
       }
     ```

```
}

const user1 = new User("john_doe", "john@example.com");
const user2 = new User("jane_doe", "jane@example.com");
console.log(user1.username); // "john_doe"
console.log(user2.username); // "jane_doe"
```

3. **Class Fields (ES2022 Update):**
   - Class fields allow direct declaration of instance properties outside the constructor:

javascript

```
class Car {
  make = "Toyota"; // Instance property
  static wheels = 4; // Static property
}

const car = new Car();
console.log(car.make); // "Toyota"
console.log(Car.wheels); // 4
```

***Practical Examples in OOP Design Patterns***

1. **Singleton Pattern:**
   - Ensures only one instance of a class is created:

     javascript

     ```
     class Singleton {
       constructor(name) {
         if (Singleton.instance) {
           return Singleton.instance;
         }
         Singleton.instance = this;
         this.name = name;
       }
     }

     const instance1 = new Singleton("Instance 1");
     const instance2 = new Singleton("Instance 2");
     console.log(instance1 === instance2); // true
     ```

2. **Factory Pattern:**
   - Creates objects without specifying the exact class:

     javascript

     ```
     class ShapeFactory {
       static createShape(type) {
     ```

```
    switch (type) {
      case "circle":
        return new Circle();
      case "square":
        return new Square();
      default:
        throw new Error("Invalid shape type");
    }
  }
}

class Circle {
  draw() {
    console.log("Drawing a circle.");
  }
}

class Square {
  draw() {
    console.log("Drawing a square.");
  }
}

const shape = ShapeFactory.createShape("circle");
shape.draw(); // "Drawing a circle."
```

3. **Observer Pattern:**
   - A pattern where objects (observers) subscribe to changes in another object (subject):

javascript

```
class Subject {
  constructor() {
    this.observers = [];
  }

  subscribe(observer) {
    this.observers.push(observer);
  }

  notify(data) {
    this.observers.forEach(observer =>
observer.update(data));
  }
}

class Observer {
  update(data) {
    console.log(`Observer received data: ${data}`);
  }
}
```

```
const subject = new Subject();
const observer1 = new Observer();
const observer2 = new Observer();

subject.subscribe(observer1);
subject.subscribe(observer2);

subject.notify("Hello, observers!");
// Observer received data: Hello, observers!
// Observer received data: Hello, observers!
```

4. **Inheritance in Frameworks:**
   - Frameworks like React use inheritance-like patterns. For example, components are defined by extending React.Component:

     javascript

```
class MyComponent extends React.Component {
  render() {
    return <h1>Hello, React!</h1>;
  }
}
```

### *Best Practices for ES6 Classes*

1. **Use Classes When OOP Fits Naturally:**
   - Use classes for scenarios where encapsulation, inheritance, and reusability are key.
2. **Prefer Composition Over Inheritance:**
   - Avoid deeply nested inheritance hierarchies; use composition for flexibility.
3. **Keep Methods Small:**
   - Break down complex functionality into smaller, reusable methods.
4. **Use Static Methods for Utilities:**
   - Place utility functions in static methods to avoid polluting instances with unnecessary functionality.
5. **Document and Type Properties:**
   - Clearly document class properties and methods, and use TypeScript for better type safety where applicable.

ES6 classes provide a powerful tool for structuring and organizing JavaScript code. With a solid understanding of their syntax and applications, you're ready to explore **Promises and asynchronous JavaScript** in the next chapter, a feature that greatly simplifies working with asynchronous operations. Let's dive in!

# CHAPTER 9: PROMISES AND ASYNCHRONOUS JAVASCRIPT

Asynchronous operations are a cornerstone of modern JavaScript, enabling non-blocking code execution for tasks like fetching data, interacting with APIs, or performing file operations. Before ES6, handling asynchronous workflows primarily relied on callbacks, which often led to complex, hard-to-maintain code known as "callback hell." ES6 introduced Promises, a game-changing feature that simplified asynchronous programming, made it more readable, and paved the way for further improvements like async/await.

In this chapter, we'll explore how Promises work, learn to chain them for clean asynchronous workflows, and compare them to traditional callbacks to highlight their advantages.

***How Promises Work: resolve, reject, and then***

A Promise is an object representing the eventual completion (or failure) of an asynchronous operation. Promises follow these core principles:

1. **States of a Promise:**
   - **Pending:** The initial state; the operation is ongoing.
   - **Fulfilled:** The operation was successful, and a value is available.
   - **Rejected:** The operation failed, and an error is available.
2. **Creating a Promise:**
   - A Promise is created using the Promise constructor, which takes a callback function with two parameters: resolve and reject.

     javascript

     ```
     const myPromise = new Promise((resolve, reject) => {
      const success = true;

      if (success) {
       resolve("Operation succeeded!");
      } else {
       reject("Operation failed!");
     ```

```
}
});

console.log(myPromise); // Promise { <pending> }
```

3. **Consuming a Promise with then and catch:**
   - Use .then() to handle a fulfilled Promise and .catch() to handle a rejected Promise:

     javascript

     ```
     myPromise
       .then(result => {
         console.log(result); // "Operation succeeded!"
       })
       .catch(error => {
         console.error(error); // "Operation failed!" (if rejected)
       });
     ```

4. **Example: Simulating an API Request:**

   javascript

   ```
   const fetchData = new Promise((resolve, reject) => {
     setTimeout(() => {
       const success = true;
   ```

```
    if (success) {
      resolve({ data: "Sample data" });
    } else {
      reject("Failed to fetch data");
    }
  }, 2000);
});

fetchData
  .then(response => {
    console.log(response.data); // "Sample data"
  })
  .catch(error => {
    console.error(error); // "Failed to fetch data"
  });
```

***Chaining Promises for Clean Asynchronous Code***

Promises can be chained to handle sequences of asynchronous operations, avoiding deeply nested callbacks.

1. **Basic Promise Chaining:**
   - Each .then() in the chain returns a new Promise, allowing operations to be performed sequentially:

     javascript

```
new Promise((resolve, reject) => {
  resolve(10);
})
  .then(result => {
    console.log(result); // 10
    return result * 2;
  })
  .then(result => {
    console.log(result); // 20
    return result + 5;
  })
  .then(result => {
    console.log(result); // 25
  })
  .catch(error => {
    console.error("Error:", error);
  });
```

2. **Handling Errors in Chains:**
   - Errors propagate down the chain, and a single .catch() can handle them:

javascript

```
new Promise((resolve, reject) => {
```

```
  reject("Something went wrong!");
})
  .then(result => {
    console.log(result); // This won't execute
  })
  .catch(error => {
    console.error(error); // "Something went wrong!"
  });
```

3. **Chaining with Dependencies:**
   - Use values from one .then() in subsequent steps:

     javascript

```
const getUser = () =>
  Promise.resolve({ id: 1, name: "John Doe" });

const getOrders = userId =>
  Promise.resolve([
    { id: 101, product: "Laptop" },
    { id: 102, product: "Phone" },
  ]);

getUser()
  .then(user => {
    console.log(user.name); // "John Doe"
```

```
  return getOrders(user.id);
})
.then(orders => {
  console.log(orders); // Orders array
})
.catch(error => {
  console.error(error);
});
```

***Comparison with Callbacks***

Promises solve many of the challenges associated with callback-based asynchronous code.

1. **Callback Hell:**
   - Callbacks often result in deeply nested code, making it hard to read and debug:

     javascript

     ```
     setTimeout(() => {
       console.log("Task 1");
       setTimeout(() => {
         console.log("Task 2");
         setTimeout(() => {
           console.log("Task 3");
     ```

```
    }, 1000);
  }, 1000);
}, 1000);
```

2. **Promise Alternative:**
   - Promises flatten the structure, improving readability:

     javascript

```
new Promise(resolve => {
  setTimeout(() => resolve("Task 1"), 1000);
})
  .then(result => {
    console.log(result);
    return new Promise(resolve => {
      setTimeout(() => resolve("Task 2"), 1000);
    });
  })
  .then(result => {
    console.log(result);
    return new Promise(resolve => {
      setTimeout(() => resolve("Task 3"), 1000);
    });
  })
  .then(result => {
    console.log(result);
```

```
});
```

3. **Error Handling:**
   - Callbacks require explicit error handling at each level, often leading to duplicated logic:

     javascript

```javascript
function fetchData(callback) {
  try {
    // Simulated API call
    const data = "Sample data";
    callback(null, data);
  } catch (error) {
    callback(error);
  }
}

fetchData((error, data) => {
  if (error) {
    console.error("Error:", error);
  } else {
    console.log(data);
  }
});
```

- Promises centralize error handling with .catch():

javascript

```
const fetchData = new Promise((resolve, reject) =>
{
 const success = true;
 success ? resolve("Sample data") : reject("Error
fetching data");
});

fetchData
 .then(data => {
  console.log(data);
 })
 .catch(error => {
  console.error("Error:", error);
 });
```

***Best Practices for Using Promises***

1. **Avoid Nesting:**
   - Use chaining instead of nesting .then() calls to keep your code flat and readable.
2. **Always Handle Errors:**

  - Attach a .catch() to handle rejections and unexpected errors gracefully.

3. **Combine Promises with Promise.all:**
   - Execute multiple Promises concurrently and wait for all to resolve:

     javascript

```
Promise.all([
  fetch("/api/users"),
  fetch("/api/orders"),
])
  .then(results => {
    console.log("Users:", results[0]);
    console.log("Orders:", results[1]);
  })
  .catch(error => {
    console.error("Error:", error);
  });
```

4. **Prefer async/await for Simplicity:**
   - Use Promises with async/await for a more synchronous-looking code structure (covered in the next chapter).

Promises simplify asynchronous code and address many of the challenges posed by traditional callbacks. In the next chapter, we'll explore **async/await**, a feature that builds on Promises to make asynchronous code even more intuitive and easier to work with. Let's continue!

# CHAPTER 10: ASYNC/AWAIT – SYNTACTIC SUGAR FOR PROMISES

While Promises revolutionized asynchronous programming in JavaScript, they can still result in verbose chains when handling sequential operations or complex error scenarios. ES2017 introduced async and await, simplifying how we work with Promises by providing a more synchronous-looking syntax for asynchronous code.

In this chapter, we'll learn how async/await works, explore error handling with try-catch, and implement real-world examples with APIs to highlight their practical benefits.

### *Writing Cleaner Asynchronous Code with Async/Await*

1. **Understanding async Functions:**

- Declaring a function with the async keyword makes it return a Promise, even if the function's body doesn't explicitly return one.

javascript

```
async function fetchData() {
  return "Data fetched!";
}

fetchData().then(result => console.log(result)); //
"Data fetched!"
```

2. **The await Keyword:**
   - await pauses the execution of an async function until the Promise resolves, allowing you to write asynchronous code in a synchronous style.

javascript

```
async function fetchData() {
  const response = await new Promise(resolve => {
    setTimeout(() => resolve("Data fetched!"),
1000);
  });
  console.log(response); // "Data fetched!"
```

```
}

fetchData();
```

3. **Sequential Promises with Async/Await:**
   - Instead of chaining .then() calls, async/await enables straightforward sequential operations:

```javascript
function fetchUser() {
  return new Promise(resolve => setTimeout(() => resolve("User data"), 1000));
}

function fetchOrders() {
  return new Promise(resolve => setTimeout(() => resolve("Order data"), 1000));
}

async function fetchAllData() {
  const user = await fetchUser();
  console.log(user); // "User data"
  const orders = await fetchOrders();
  console.log(orders); // "Order data"
}
```

```
fetchAllData();
```

4. **Concurrency with await:**
   - To run multiple asynchronous operations concurrently, use Promise.all:

```javascript
async function fetchConcurrent() {
  const [user, orders] = await Promise.all([fetchUser(), fetchOrders()]);
  console.log(user); // "User data"
  console.log(orders); // "Order data"
}

fetchConcurrent();
```

### *Error Handling with Try-Catch*

1. **Basic Error Handling:**
   - Errors in an async function are automatically rejected as Promises. Use try-catch for clean error handling:

javascript

```
async function fetchData() {
  try {
    const response = await new Promise((resolve, reject) =>
      setTimeout(() => reject("Fetch failed!"), 1000)
    );
    console.log(response);
  } catch (error) {
    console.error("Error:", error); // "Error: Fetch failed!"
  }
}

fetchData();
```

2. **Nested Try-Catch Blocks:**
   - Use separate try-catch blocks for granular error handling:

javascript

```
async function fetchData() {
  try {
    const user = await fetchUser();
    try {
```

```
    const orders = await fetchOrders();
    console.log(orders);
   } catch (orderError) {
    console.error("Failed to fetch orders:", orderError);
   }
  } catch (userError) {
   console.error("Failed to fetch user:", userError);
  }
}

fetchData();
```

3. **Combining Try-Catch with .catch:**
   - Alternatively, you can use .catch for handling errors when calling an async function:

javascript

```javascript
async function fetchData() {
 const response = await fetch("https://invalid-url.com");
 return response.json();
}
```

```
fetchData().catch(error => console.error("Fetch error:", error));
```

### *Real-World Examples with APIs*

1. **Fetching Data from an API:**
   - Use async/await to make API requests straightforward and readable:

```javascript
async function fetchUserData() {
  try {
    const response = await fetch("https://jsonplaceholder.typicode.com/users/1");
    const data = await response.json();
    console.log(data); // User object
  } catch (error) {
    console.error("Error fetching user data:", error);
  }
}

fetchUserData();
```

2. **Chaining API Requests:**

- Combine multiple API requests by awaiting them sequentially:

javascript

```
async function fetchUserAndPosts() {
  try {
    const userResponse = await fetch("https://jsonplaceholder.typicode.com/users/1");
    const user = await userResponse.json();
    console.log("User:", user);

    const postsResponse = await fetch("https://jsonplaceholder.typicode.com/posts?userId=1");
    const posts = await postsResponse.json();
    console.log("Posts:", posts);
  } catch (error) {
    console.error("Error:", error);
  }
}

fetchUserAndPosts();
```

3. **Retry Mechanism:**

- Implement a retry mechanism for network requests:

javascript

```
async function fetchWithRetry(url, retries = 3) {
  while (retries > 0) {
    try {
      const response = await fetch(url);
      if (!response.ok) throw new Error("HTTP error");
      return await response.json();
    } catch (error) {
      console.error("Attempt failed:", error);
      retries--;
      if (retries === 0) throw new Error("All attempts failed");
    }
  }
}

fetchWithRetry("https://jsonplaceholder.typicode.com/posts/1")
  .then(data => console.log("Data:", data))
  .catch(error => console.error("Final Error:", error));
```

### *Best Practices for Using Async/Await*

1. **Always Handle Errors:**
   - Wrap await calls in try-catch blocks or attach .catch to handle rejected Promises.
2. **Combine Async/Await with Promise.all:**
   - Use Promise.all for concurrent operations to improve performance.
3. **Avoid Blocking the Event Loop:**
   - Avoid long await operations in critical parts of the code, as they can block execution.
4. **Keep Functions Focused:**
   - Break down large async functions into smaller, reusable pieces for better readability and testing.
5. **Leverage Libraries:**
   - Use libraries like axios for improved Promise-based HTTP handling with built-in error handling and interceptors.

With async/await, asynchronous programming in JavaScript becomes more intuitive and readable, making it easier to manage complex workflows. In the next chapter, we'll explore **modules in ES6**, which revolutionized how JavaScript handles imports and exports, enabling better code organization and maintainability. Let's continue!

# CHAPTER 11: MODULES IN ES6

Modules are essential for organizing and managing code in modern JavaScript applications. Before ES6, developers relied on module systems like CommonJS or AMD to achieve modularity. With ES6, JavaScript introduced native module syntax, providing a standardized way to import and export functionality across files.

In this chapter, we'll explore how to use ES6 modules, compare them to CommonJS, and learn how to set up module-based applications.

### *Importing and Exporting with ES6 Modules*

1. **Exporting in ES6 Modules:**

- **Named Exports:** Export multiple entities from a module by name.

  javascript

  ```
  // math.js
  export const add = (a, b) => a + b;
  export const subtract = (a, b) => a - b;
  ```

- **Default Exports:** Export a single default entity, typically used for the primary functionality of a module.

  javascript

  ```
  // logger.js
  export default function log(message) {
    console.log(message);
  }
  ```

2. **Importing in ES6 Modules:**
   - Import named exports by their exact names.

     javascript

     ```
     // app.js
     import { add, subtract } from './math.js';
     ```

```
console.log(add(5, 3)); // 8
console.log(subtract(5, 3)); // 2
```

- Import default exports using any name.

javascript

```
// app.js
import log from './logger.js';

log("Hello, ES6 Modules!"); // "Hello, ES6 Modules!"
```

- Combine named and default imports.

javascript

```
import log, { add } from './math.js';

log(add(5, 3)); // "8"
```

3. **Re-exporting from Modules:**
    - Re-exporting allows modules to consolidate exports from other modules:

javascript

```
// utility.js
export { add, subtract } from './math.js';
export { default as log } from './logger.js';

// app.js
import { add, log } from './utility.js';
```

4. **Dynamic Imports:**
   - Load modules dynamically using import(), which returns a Promise:

     javascript

     ```
     async function loadMath() {
       const { add } = await import('./math.js');
       console.log(add(2, 3)); // 5
     }

     loadMath();
     ```

### ***Differences Between CommonJS and ES6 Modules***

1. **Syntax Differences:**
   - **CommonJS:**

- Exports functionality using module.exports or exports.

javascript

```
// math.js (CommonJS)
exports.add = (a, b) => a + b;
```

- Imports using require.

javascript

```
const { add } = require('./math.js');
```

- **ES6 Modules:**
  - Uses export and import keywords.

javascript

```
export const add = (a, b) => a + b;
import { add } from './math.js';
```

2. **Default Export Handling:**
   - In CommonJS, module.exports can be assigned directly:

javascript

```
module.exports = function log(message) {
  console.log(message);
};
const log = require('./logger.js');
```

- ES6 Modules use export default.

3. **Synchronous vs. Asynchronous Loading:**
   - CommonJS modules are loaded synchronously, making them better suited for server-side Node.js applications.
   - ES6 modules are loaded asynchronously, making them ideal for client-side applications and browser environments.
4. **Browser Compatibility:**
   - CommonJS modules require a bundler like Webpack for browser usage.
   - ES6 modules are natively supported in modern browsers when using <script type="module">.
5. **Scope and Execution:**
   - CommonJS modules execute at runtime, and their exports are mutable.
   - ES6 modules are static, allowing better optimizations like tree-shaking and improved performance.

### *Setting Up Module-Based Applications*

1. **Browser Environment:**
   - Use <script type="module"> to enable ES6 modules in the browser:

     html

     ```html
     <!-- index.html -->
     <script type="module" src="app.js"></script>
     ```

   - Modules are loaded with relative or absolute paths:

     javascript

     ```javascript
     // app.js
     import { add } from './math.js';
     console.log(add(1, 2)); // 3
     ```

2. **Node.js Environment:**
   - Enable ES6 modules by setting "type": "module" in package.json:

     json

     ```json
     {
     ```

```
  "type": "module"
}
```

- Use .js extensions for module imports:

```javascript
import { add } from './math.js';
```

3. **Using Bundlers:**
   - For large applications, use tools like Webpack or Rollup to bundle modules for production:
     - Install Webpack:

```bash
npm install webpack webpack-cli --save-dev
```

     - Configure Webpack to handle ES6 modules:

```javascript
// webpack.config.js
module.exports = {
  entry: './src/app.js',
  output: {
    filename: 'bundle.js',
```

```
      path: __dirname + '/dist',
    },
    module: {
      rules: [
        {
          test: /\.js$/,
          exclude: /node_modules/,
          use: {
            loader: 'babel-loader',
          },
        },
      ],
    },
  };
```

4. **Organizing Modules in Applications:**
   - Structure your project with clear module boundaries:

```css

src/
├── components/
│   ├── header.js
│   └── footer.js
├── services/
│   ├── api.js
```

```
│   └── auth.js
├── utils/
│   └── helper.js
└── app.js
```

- Example app.js:

  javascript

  ```javascript
  import { fetchUser } from './services/api.js';
  import { authenticate } from './services/auth.js';
  import { log } from './utils/helper.js';

  async function main() {
   const user = await fetchUser();
   authenticate(user);
   log("User authenticated");
  }

  main();
  ```

### *Best Practices for ES6 Modules*

1. **Use Named Exports for Multiple Entities:**
   - Use named exports when a module provides multiple related utilities:

```javascript
export const add = (a, b) => a + b;
export const subtract = (a, b) => a - b;
```

2. **Use Default Exports for Primary Functions:**
   - Use default exports when the module has a clear primary responsibility:

   ```javascript
   export default function log(message) {
     console.log(message);
   }
   ```

3. **Keep Module Scope Clean:**
   - Avoid polluting the global scope; ensure each module encapsulates its functionality.
4. **Organize by Features:**
   - Structure modules by features or domains rather than generic categories.
5. **Leverage Tree-Shaking:**
   - Only import what you need to minimize bundle size:

   ```javascript
   import { specificFunction } from './largeModule.js';
   ```

ES6 modules revolutionized how JavaScript manages code modularity, promoting clean, maintainable, and scalable applications. In the next chapter, we'll explore **iterators and generators**, essential tools for handling sequential data and lazy evaluation. Let's dive in!

# CHAPTER 12: ITERATORS AND GENERATORS

Iterators and generators are fundamental concepts in JavaScript for managing sequential data and asynchronous workflows. Introduced in ES6, they allow developers to traverse collections, build custom iteration logic, and implement lazy evaluation with ease.

In this chapter, we'll dive into the concept of iterators, learn how to create custom iterators, explore the for...of loop, and discover how generators can simplify handling complex data flows, including asynchronous operations.

### *The Concept of Iterators in JavaScript*

1. **What is an Iterator?**

- An iterator is an object that provides a way to traverse a sequence of values, one value at a time. It implements the next() method, which returns:
  - { value: <value>, done: false } when there are more values to yield.
  - { value: undefined, done: true } when the sequence is complete.

2. **Built-in Iterators:**
   - JavaScript collections like arrays, strings, maps, and sets have built-in iterators accessible via the Symbol.iterator property.

javascript

```
const array = [1, 2, 3];
const iterator = array[Symbol.iterator]();

console.log(iterator.next()); // { value: 1, done: false }
console.log(iterator.next()); // { value: 2, done: false }
console.log(iterator.next()); // { value: 3, done: false }
console.log(iterator.next()); // { value: undefined, done: true }
```

3. **Why Iterators Matter:**
   - Iterators provide a consistent interface for working with sequential data, regardless of the underlying data structure.

***Writing Custom Iterators and Using for...of***

1. **Custom Iterators:**
   - Create custom iterators by defining an object with a next() method:

     javascript

     ```
     const range = {
      start: 1,
      end: 5,
      current: 1,
      [Symbol.iterator]() {
       return this;
      },
      next() {
       if (this.current <= this.end) {
        return { value: this.current++, done: false };
       }
       return { value: undefined, done: true };
      },
     ```

```
};

for (const num of range) {
  console.log(num); // 1, 2, 3, 4, 5
}
```

2. **Using for...of:**
   - The for...of loop simplifies iterating over iterable objects like arrays, strings, maps, sets, and custom iterators:

```javascript
const fruits = ["apple", "banana", "cherry"];
for (const fruit of fruits) {
  console.log(fruit);
}
```

3. **Iterating Over Non-Array Objects:**
   - Example with a Map:

```javascript
const map = new Map([
  ["name", "Alice"],
  ["age", 25],
]);
```

```
for (const [key, value] of map) {
  console.log(`${key}: ${value}`);
}
```

***Generators for Lazy Evaluation and Asynchronous Workflows***

1. **What is a Generator?**
   - A generator is a special type of function defined with function*. It can pause its execution using yield and resume later, allowing for lazy evaluation.

     javascript

```
function* generatorFunction() {
  yield 1;
  yield 2;
  yield 3;
}

const generator = generatorFunction();

console.log(generator.next()); // { value: 1, done: false }
```

```
console.log(generator.next()); // { value: 2, done: false }
console.log(generator.next()); // { value: 3, done: false }
console.log(generator.next()); // { value: undefined, done: true }
```

2. **Lazy Evaluation:**
   - Generators compute values only when requested, optimizing memory usage for large or infinite sequences.

javascript

```
function* infiniteSequence() {
  let i = 1;
  while (true) {
    yield i++;
  }
}

const sequence = infiniteSequence();
console.log(sequence.next().value); // 1
console.log(sequence.next().value); // 2
```

3. **Combining Generators with Iterators:**

- Generators simplify custom iterator implementation:

```javascript
function* range(start, end) {
  for (let i = start; i <= end; i++) {
    yield i;
  }
}

for (const num of range(1, 5)) {
  console.log(num); // 1, 2, 3, 4, 5
}
```

4. **Generators for Asynchronous Workflows:**
   - Generators can manage asynchronous operations when combined with Promises:

```javascript
function* fetchGenerator() {
  yield
fetch("https://jsonplaceholder.typicode.com/posts/1
").then(res => res.json());
```

```
 yield
fetch("https://jsonplaceholder.typicode.com/posts/2
").then(res => res.json());
}

const generator = fetchGenerator();

generator.next().value.then(data =>
console.log(data));
generator.next().value.then(data =>
console.log(data));
```

### *Practical Applications of Iterators and Generators*

1. **Data Streaming:**
   - Use generators to process streaming data in chunks.

   javascript

```
function* chunkGenerator(array, size) {
  for (let i = 0; i < array.length; i += size) {
    yield array.slice(i, i + size);
  }
}
```

```
const chunks = chunkGenerator([1, 2, 3, 4, 5, 6], 2);
console.log(chunks.next().value); // [1, 2]
console.log(chunks.next().value); // [3, 4]
```

2. **Pagination:**
   - Fetch paginated data lazily using a generator:

     javascript

```
async function* paginatedFetch(url, totalPages) {
  for (let page = 1; page <= totalPages; page++) {
    const response = await fetch(`${url}?page=${page}`);
    const data = await response.json();
    yield data;
  }
}

(async () => {
  const pages = paginatedFetch("https://api.example.com/items", 3);
  for await (const page of pages) {
    console.log(page);
  }
})();
```

3. **Custom Iterables:**
   - Define domain-specific collections with built-in iteration:

     javascript

     ```
     class Fibonacci {
      constructor(limit) {
       this.limit = limit;
      }

      *[Symbol.iterator]() {
       let [prev, curr] = [0, 1];
       for (let i = 0; i < this.limit; i++) {
        yield curr;
        [prev, curr] = [curr, prev + curr];
       }
      }
     }

     for (const num of new Fibonacci(5)) {
      console.log(num); // 1, 1, 2, 3, 5
     }
     ```

***Best Practices for Iterators and Generators***

1. **Use for...of for Readability:**
    - Prefer for...of over manually iterating with .next() unless custom logic is required.
2. **Leverage Generators for Lazy Evaluation:**
    - Use generators for scenarios where data is produced incrementally, such as infinite sequences or large datasets.
3. **Combine with Promises for Async Workflows:**
    - Generators work seamlessly with Promises to manage asynchronous tasks in a structured manner.
4. **Keep Iterators and Generators Focused:**
    - Ensure iterators and generators have a single responsibility to maintain clarity.

Iterators and generators add significant flexibility for handling sequential and asynchronous workflows in JavaScript. In the next chapter, we'll explore **Maps and Sets**, two powerful ES6 data structures that simplify working with collections. Let's continue!

# CHAPTER 13: THE ES6 MAP AND SET DATA STRUCTURES

ES6 introduced two powerful data structures, Map and Set, along with their weak counterparts, WeakMap and WeakSet. These additions addressed limitations of traditional objects and arrays in specific scenarios, offering better performance, memory optimization, and specialized use cases.

In this chapter, we'll explore the advantages of Map and Set, understand how WeakMap and WeakSet optimize memory management, and dive into practical applications like caching and data deduplication.

### *Advantages of Map and Set over Traditional Objects and Arrays*

1. **Map:**
   - A Map is a collection of key-value pairs, where keys can be of any data type (not limited to strings or symbols like object keys).

     javascript

     ```
     const map = new Map();
     map.set(1, "one");
     map.set("two", 2);
     console.log(map.get(1)); // "one"
     console.log(map.get("two")); // 2
     ```

   - **Advantages Over Objects:**
     - **Key Flexibility:** Keys can be any type, including objects, functions, or primitives.
     - **Iteration Order:** Map maintains the order of entries.
     - **Performance:** Optimized for frequent additions, deletions, and lookups compared to objects.
     - **Size Property:** Easily retrieve the number of entries using .size:

       javascript

```
console.log(map.size); // 2
```

2. **Set:**
   - A Set is a collection of unique values, ensuring no duplicates.

     javascript

     ```
     const set = new Set();
     set.add(1);
     set.add(1); // Duplicate, won't be added
     set.add(2);
     console.log(set); // Set { 1, 2 }
     ```

   - **Advantages Over Arrays:**
     - **Uniqueness:** Automatically removes duplicates, simplifying operations like deduplication.
     - **Efficiency:** Faster lookups and removals for large collections compared to arrays.
     - **Iteration Order:** Preserves the order of insertion.
     - **Size Property:** Quickly get the size of the set:

       javascript

```
console.log(set.size); // 2
```

### *WeakMap and WeakSet for Memory Optimization*

1. **WeakMap:**
   - A WeakMap is similar to a Map but only accepts objects as keys and holds them weakly. This means the keys can be garbage collected when no other references exist, preventing memory leaks.

     javascript

     ```
     let obj = { id: 1 };
     const weakMap = new WeakMap();
     weakMap.set(obj, "value");

     console.log(weakMap.get(obj)); // "value"
     obj = null; // The key-value pair is now eligible for garbage collection.
     ```

   - **Use Cases:**
     - Storing metadata for DOM elements or objects without preventing their garbage collection.
2. **WeakSet:**

- A WeakSet only stores objects and holds them weakly, allowing them to be garbage collected if there are no other references.

```javascript
let user = { name: "John" };
const weakSet = new WeakSet();
weakSet.add(user);

console.log(weakSet.has(user)); // true
user = null; // The object is now eligible for garbage collection.
```

- **Use Cases:**
  - Tracking objects without creating memory leaks, such as keeping a reference to objects for monitoring purposes.

3. **Limitations of WeakMap and WeakSet:**
   - No size property or iteration: They are designed for cases where the keys or objects should not prevent garbage collection, so they lack enumeration capabilities.

### ***Practical Examples in Caching and Data Deduplication***

1. **Caching with Map:**
   - Efficiently store and retrieve computed or fetched results.

     javascript

```
const cache = new Map();

function fetchData(key) {
  if (cache.has(key)) {
    console.log("Returning from cache");
    return cache.get(key);
  }

  const value = `Data for ${key}`; // Simulate data
fetching
  cache.set(key, value);
  console.log("Fetched and cached");
  return value;
}

console.log(fetchData("user1")); // Fetched and
cached
console.log(fetchData("user1")); // Returning from
cache
```

2. **Tracking DOM Elements with WeakMap:**
   - Use WeakMap to associate metadata with DOM elements, avoiding memory leaks.

     javascript

     ```
     const elementMetadata = new WeakMap();

     const div = document.createElement("div");
     elementMetadata.set(div, { clicked: false });

     div.addEventListener("click", () => {
       const meta = elementMetadata.get(div);
       meta.clicked = true;
       console.log("Div clicked!");
     });
     ```

3. **Deduplication with Set:**
   - Automatically remove duplicates from an array:

     javascript

     ```
     const numbers = [1, 2, 2, 3, 4, 4, 5];
     const uniqueNumbers = [...new Set(numbers)];
     console.log(uniqueNumbers); // [1, 2, 3, 4, 5]
     ```

4. **Object Tracking with WeakSet:**

- Monitor live objects, such as user connections:

  ```javascript
  const activeUsers = new WeakSet();

  let user1 = { name: "Alice" };
  let user2 = { name: "Bob" };

  activeUsers.add(user1);
  activeUsers.add(user2);

  console.log(activeUsers.has(user1)); // true
  user1 = null; // Automatically garbage collected.
  ```

5. **Frequency Counting with Map:**
   - Count the occurrence of elements in an array:

     ```javascript
     const items = ["apple", "banana", "apple", "orange",
     "banana"];
     const frequency = new Map();

     for (const item of items) {
       frequency.set(item, (frequency.get(item) || 0) + 1);
     ```

```
}

console.log(frequency); // Map { 'apple' => 2, 'banana' => 2, 'orange' => 1 }
```

### *Best Practices for Using Map and Set*

1. **Choose the Right Data Structure:**
   - Use Map for key-value pairs where keys may not be strings.
   - Use Set for collections of unique values.
2. **Leverage WeakMap and WeakSet for Memory-Sensitive Applications:**
   - Use WeakMap and WeakSet to store metadata or track objects without causing memory leaks.
3. **Avoid Overusing WeakMap and WeakSet:**
   - Their non-iterable nature makes them unsuitable for general-purpose use.
4. **Use Spread and Destructuring:**
   - Combine Set and Map with modern JavaScript features for concise and readable code:

     javascript

```
const map = new Map([["key1", "value1"], ["key2",
"value2"]]);
const keys = [...map.keys()];
console.log(keys); // ['key1', 'key2']
```

Maps and Sets offer performance and flexibility improvements over traditional objects and arrays, while their weak counterparts are indispensable for memory-sensitive use cases. In the next chapter, we'll explore **Symbols**, another ES6 feature that introduces unique, immutable values ideal for creating private properties and managing collisions in object keys. Let's continue!

# CHAPTER 14: THE SYMBOL PRIMITIVE

The Symbol primitive in ES6 introduced a way to create unique, immutable values in JavaScript. Symbols play a critical role in object property management and provide a mechanism to avoid property name collisions, especially in environments like libraries or frameworks. Symbols also power key JavaScript internals through well-known Symbol properties.

In this chapter, we'll explore the concept of Symbols, learn how to use them as unique identifiers, and discuss practical applications in object property management.

### *Understanding the Role of Symbols in ES6*

1. **What Are Symbols?**
   - A Symbol is a unique and immutable primitive value introduced in ES6.
   - Unlike strings, every Symbol is guaranteed to be unique, even if created with the same description.

```javascript
const sym1 = Symbol("description");
const sym2 = Symbol("description");

console.log(sym1 === sym2); // false
```

2. **Why Use Symbols?**
   - Prevent name collisions in objects, particularly when integrating third-party libraries or frameworks.
   - Define properties that won't accidentally conflict with other keys in objects.
   - Enable private-like properties in objects by making them non-enumerable.
3. **Symbol as a Primitive:**

- Symbols are one of JavaScript's seven primitive types and can be created using the Symbol() function.
- They cannot be constructed with new:

```javascript
const sym = Symbol(); // Valid
const sym2 = new Symbol(); // TypeError
```

4. **Symbol Descriptions:**
   - While Symbols are unique, you can provide an optional description to help with debugging:

```javascript
const sym = Symbol("uniqueKey");
console.log(sym.description); // "uniqueKey"
```

***Using Symbols for Unique Identifiers***

1. **Symbols as Object Keys:**
   - Symbols can be used as keys for object properties, ensuring uniqueness and preventing accidental overwrites:

```javascript
const sym = Symbol("id");
const user = {
  [sym]: 1234,
  name: "Alice",
};

console.log(user[sym]); // 1234
```

2. **Symbols and Iteration:**
   - Properties with Symbol keys are not enumerable, meaning they won't appear in loops like for...in or Object.keys():

```javascript
const sym = Symbol("hidden");
const obj = {
  visible: "I am visible",
  [sym]: "I am hidden",
};

console.log(Object.keys(obj)); // ["visible"]
console.log(obj[sym]); // "I am hidden"
```

3. **Global Symbols:**
   - Use Symbol.for to create or access a global Symbol. This ensures a shared Symbol instance across your application:

     javascript

     ```
     const globalSym1 = Symbol.for("shared");
     const globalSym2 = Symbol.for("shared");

     console.log(globalSym1 === globalSym2); // true
     ```
   - Retrieve the key for a global Symbol:

     javascript

     ```
     console.log(Symbol.keyFor(globalSym1)); // "shared"
     ```

### *Application in Object Property Management*

1. **Defining Private-Like Properties:**
   - Use Symbols to create properties that are inaccessible through standard enumeration or property access:

javascript

```
const _id = Symbol("id");
const user = {
  [_id]: 1234,
  name: "Alice",
};

console.log(user[_id]); // 1234
```

2. **Avoiding Key Collisions:**
   - Use Symbols to define unique keys in objects that integrate with third-party code:

javascript

```
const libraryKey = Symbol("libKey");

const config = {
  [libraryKey]: "Library-specific setting",
  global: "Global setting",
};

console.log(config[libraryKey]); // "Library-specific setting"
```

3. **Well-Known Symbols:**
   - JavaScript includes built-in Symbols (well-known Symbols) to customize object behavior:
     - Symbol.iterator: Define custom iteration behavior.
     - Symbol.toStringTag: Control the default string representation of an object.
     - Symbol.hasInstance: Customize instanceof checks.

Example with Symbol.iterator:

```javascript
const iterable = {
  *[Symbol.iterator]() {
    yield 1;
    yield 2;
    yield 3;
  },
};

for (const value of iterable) {
  console.log(value); // 1, 2, 3
}
```

4. **Tagging Classes and Objects:**
   - Use Symbol.toStringTag to customize the output of Object.prototype.toString:

```javascript
class CustomClass {
  get [Symbol.toStringTag]() {
    return "CustomClass";
  }
}

const obj = new CustomClass();
console.log(Object.prototype.toString.call(obj)); // "[object CustomClass]"
```

5. **Event Emitters:**
   - Use Symbols to define event keys to avoid collisions in event management systems:

```javascript
const EVENT_UPDATE = Symbol("update");

class EventEmitter {
  constructor() {
```

```
    this.events = {};
  }

  on(event, callback) {
    this.events[event] = callback;
  }

  emit(event, data) {
    if (this.events[event]) {
      this.events[event](data);
    }
  }
}

const emitter = new EventEmitter();
emitter.on(EVENT_UPDATE, data =>
console.log("Update received:", data));
emitter.emit(EVENT_UPDATE, { id: 1 });
```

***Best Practices for Using Symbols***

1. **Use Descriptions for Debugging:**
    - Always provide a description to improve readability and debugging.
2. **Leverage Global Symbols for Shared Keys:**

    - Use Symbol.for for keys that need to be reused across modules or libraries.
3. **Combine Symbols with Well-Known Symbols:**
    - Customize default behaviors for advanced use cases like iteration or type-checking.
4. **Avoid Overusing Symbols:**
    - Symbols are ideal for specialized scenarios like unique keys or private properties. Use strings for general-purpose keys for better readability.

Symbols provide a unique mechanism for handling object properties and managing collisions in JavaScript. They are especially useful in library development and internal data structures. In the next chapter, we'll explore **default, rest, and spread in function parameters**, enhancing how we handle dynamic arguments and defaults in JavaScript functions. Let's continue!

# CHAPTER 15: DEFAULT, REST, AND SPREAD IN FUNCTION PARAMETERS

JavaScript functions gained powerful enhancements in ES6 with default parameters, rest parameters, and the spread operator. These features simplify function definitions, improve flexibility, and reduce boilerplate, making functions more expressive and versatile.

In this chapter, we'll explore how to set default values for function parameters, use rest parameters to handle dynamic arguments, and leverage the spread operator to pass flexible arguments into functions.

### *Setting Default Values for Function Parameters*

Default parameters allow you to specify default values for function arguments, ensuring that a function works even when some arguments are omitted.

1. **Basic Syntax:**
   - Use the = operator to define default values for parameters:

     javascript

     ```
     function greet(name = "Guest") {
       console.log(`Hello, ${name}!`);
     }

     greet(); // "Hello, Guest!"
     greet("Alice"); // "Hello, Alice!"
     ```

2. **Dynamic Defaults:**

- Default values can be expressions or the result of other function calls:

  javascript

  ```
  function generateId() {
    return Math.random().toString(36).substring(2, 8);
  }

  function createUser(username = `User-${generateId()}`) {
    console.log(`Welcome, ${username}`);
  }

  createUser(); // "Welcome, User-xxxxxx" (random ID)
  createUser("Alice"); // "Welcome, Alice"
  ```

3. **Order of Defaults:**
   - Default values depend on parameters defined earlier:

     javascript

     ```
     function calculatePrice(price, tax = price * 0.1) {
       return price + tax;
     }
     ```

```
console.log(calculatePrice(100)); // 110
console.log(calculatePrice(100, 15)); // 115
```

4. **Avoiding Undefined Values:**
   - Default parameters prevent bugs caused by missing arguments:

     javascript

     ```
     function log(message = "No message provided") {
       console.log(message);
     }

     log(); // "No message provided"
     log(undefined); // "No message provided"
     log(null); // "null"
     ```

***Using Rest Parameters for Dynamic Arguments***

Rest parameters allow a function to accept an indefinite number of arguments as an array, making it easier to handle flexible inputs.

1. **Basic Syntax:**
   - Use the ... syntax to collect remaining arguments into an array:

javascript

```
function sum(...numbers) {
 return numbers.reduce((total, num) => total + num, 0);
}

console.log(sum(1, 2, 3, 4)); // 10
console.log(sum(5, 10)); // 15
```

2. **Combining Rest Parameters with Fixed Arguments:**
   - Rest parameters must appear at the end of the parameter list:

     javascript

```
function describePerson(name, age, ...hobbies) {
 console.log(`${name} is ${age} years old and enjoys: ${hobbies.join(", ")}`);
}

describePerson("Alice", 30, "reading", "cycling", "cooking");
// "Alice is 30 years old and enjoys: reading, cycling, cooking"
```

3. **Destructuring with Rest:**
   - Rest parameters can be combined with destructuring:

     javascript

     ```
     function splitArray([first, second, ...rest]) {
       console.log(`First: ${first}, Second: ${second}, Rest: ${rest}`);
     }

     splitArray([1, 2, 3, 4, 5]); // "First: 1, Second: 2, Rest: 3,4,5"
     ```

4. **Replacing arguments:**
   - Rest parameters are a cleaner alternative to the arguments object:

     javascript

     ```
     function logAll(...args) {
       console.log(args);
     }

     logAll(1, "hello", true); // [1, "hello", true]
     ```

***Combining Spread with Functions for Flexibility***

The spread operator (...) expands an array or object into individual elements, making it easier to pass arguments dynamically into functions.

1. **Passing Arrays as Arguments:**
   - Spread an array into individual arguments:

     javascript

     ```
     const numbers = [10, 20, 30];
     console.log(Math.max(...numbers)); // 30
     ```

2. **Combining with Rest Parameters:**
   - Use spread to combine arrays and handle flexible inputs:

     javascript

     ```
     function combineArrays(...arrays) {
       return [].concat(...arrays);
     }

     const result = combineArrays([1, 2], [3, 4], [5]);
     console.log(result); // [1, 2, 3, 4, 5]
     ```

3. **Merging Arguments Dynamically:**
   - Spread allows dynamic argument creation:

```javascript
const baseArgs = [100, 0.2];
const finalPrice = calculatePrice(...baseArgs); //
calculatePrice(price, tax)
console.log(finalPrice); // 120
```

4. **Creating Flexible Function Wrappers:**
   - Spread is useful for wrapping functions:

```javascript
function logger(...args) {
  console.log(...args);
}

const data = ["Log this", "and this", "too"];
logger(...data); // "Log this and this too"
```

5. **Handling Default and Spread Together:**
   - Combine default parameters with spread for robust functions:

```javascript
function createList(title = "Untitled", ...items) {
  console.log(`${title}: ${items.join(", ")}`);
```

```
}

createList("Groceries", "Milk", "Eggs", "Bread");
// "Groceries: Milk, Eggs, Bread"

createList(); // "Untitled: "
```

***Practical Examples***

1. **Custom Summation Function:**

javascript

```
function customSum(base = 0, ...numbers) {
  return numbers.reduce((total, num) => total + num, base);
}

console.log(customSum(10, 1, 2, 3)); // 16
console.log(customSum()); // 0
```

2. **Flexible Logging Utility:**

javascript

```
function logDetails(prefix = "[LOG]", ...messages) {
  console.log(`${prefix} ${messages.join(" ")}`);
```

```
}

logDetails("INFO", "Server started", "at port 3000");
// "INFO Server started at port 3000"
```

3. **Dynamic Argument Combination:**

javascript

```
function mergeAndCalculate(multiplier, ...arrays) {
  const combined = [].concat(...arrays);
  return combined.map(num => num * multiplier);
}

console.log(mergeAndCalculate(2, [1, 2], [3, 4]));
// [2, 4, 6, 8]
```

4. **RESTful API Data Builder:**

javascript

```
function buildRequest(method = "GET", endpoint,
...params) {
  return {
    method,
    url: `${endpoint}?${params.join("&")}`,
  };
```

```
}

const request = buildRequest("POST", "/api/resource",
"id=1", "type=user");
console.log(request);
// { method: "POST", url: "/api/resource?id=1&type=user"
}
```

*Best Practices*

1. **Use Default Parameters for Robust Functions:**
   - Provide defaults for optional parameters to reduce error handling.
2. **Leverage Rest Parameters for Clean Dynamic Inputs:**
   - Prefer rest parameters over manual handling of arguments for readability and maintainability.
3. **Use Spread for Flexibility:**
   - Spread simplifies argument passing and dynamic array manipulation.
4. **Combine Features for Comprehensive Solutions:**
   - Combine default, rest, and spread for advanced function design:

     javascript

```
function processEntries(title = "Data", ...entries) {
  console.log(`${title}: ${entries.join(", ")}`);
}

const data = [1, 2, 3];
processEntries("Numbers", ...data);
// "Numbers: 1, 2, 3"
```

Default parameters, rest, and spread make JavaScript functions more dynamic, readable, and efficient. In the next chapter, we'll explore **Proxies and the Reflect API**, two advanced tools that enable meta-programming and dynamic behavior in JavaScript. Let's continue!

# CHAPTER 16: THE ES6 PROXY AND REFLECT API

The introduction of Proxies and the Reflect API in ES6 brought a new level of flexibility and control to JavaScript. Proxies allow developers to intercept and customize fundamental operations on objects, such as property access, assignment, and function invocation. The Reflect API complements Proxies by providing methods to perform default object operations in a consistent, structured way.

In this chapter, we'll learn how to create Proxy objects for dynamic behavior, explore the Reflect API for meta-programming, and examine real-world examples, including data validation and logging.

### *Creating Proxy Objects for Dynamic Behavior*

A Proxy is an object that wraps another object (the target) and intercepts operations performed on it. This allows customization of behavior for property access, assignment, deletion, and more.

1. **Basic Syntax:**
   - Create a Proxy by passing a target object and a handler object containing traps (interception functions):

     javascript

     ```
     const target = { name: "Alice", age: 25 };
     const handler = {
       get(obj, prop) {
     ```

```
    console.log(`Accessing property: ${prop}`);
    return obj[prop];
  },
};

const proxy = new Proxy(target, handler);
console.log(proxy.name); // Logs: "Accessing property: name", Outputs: "Alice"
```

2. **Common Traps in Proxies:**
   - **get:** Intercept property access.

javascript

```
const handler = {
  get(obj, prop) {
    return prop in obj ? obj[prop] : "Property does not exist";
  },
};
```

   - **set:** Intercept property assignment.

javascript

```
const handler = {
  set(obj, prop, value) {
```

```
    if (prop === "age" && typeof value !== "number") {
      throw new TypeError("Age must be a number");
    }
    obj[prop] = value;
    return true;
  },
};
```

- **deleteProperty:** Intercept property deletion.

javascript

```
const handler = {
  deleteProperty(obj, prop) {
    console.log(`Deleting property: ${prop}`);
    delete obj[prop];
    return true;
  },
};
```

- **apply:** Intercept function calls.

javascript

```
const handler = {
  apply(target, thisArg, args) {
```

```
    console.log(`Function called with arguments: ${args}`);
    return target(...args);
  },
};
```

3. **Example: Read-Only Object:**
   - Create a proxy that prevents modifications to an object:

javascript

```javascript
const target = { name: "Alice", age: 25 };
const handler = {
  set() {
    throw new Error("Modifications are not allowed");
  },
};

const readOnlyProxy = new Proxy(target, handler);
console.log(readOnlyProxy.name); // "Alice"
readOnlyProxy.age = 30; // Error: Modifications are not allowed
```

### *Using the Reflect API for Meta-Programming*

The Reflect API provides a set of static methods for performing object operations, such as property access, assignment, and function application, in a consistent and predictable way.

1. **Reflect API Basics:**
    - Reflect methods are direct counterparts to many built-in object operations:

      javascript

      ```
      const obj = { name: "Alice" };

      // Using Reflect to access properties
      console.log(Reflect.get(obj, "name")); // "Alice"

      // Using Reflect to set properties
      Reflect.set(obj, "age", 25);
      console.log(obj.age); // 25

      // Using Reflect to delete properties
      Reflect.deleteProperty(obj, "name");
      console.log(obj.name); // undefined
      ```

2. **Common Reflect Methods:**
    - **Reflect.get:** Retrieve a property value.

- **Reflect.set:** Set a property value.
- **Reflect.has:** Check if a property exists (like the in operator).

javascript

```
console.log(Reflect.has(obj, "age")); // true
```

- **Reflect.deleteProperty:** Delete a property.
- **Reflect.apply:** Call a function with arguments.

javascript

```
const sum = (a, b) => a + b;
console.log(Reflect.apply(sum, null, [5, 3])); // 8
```

- **Reflect.ownKeys:** Get all property keys (including Symbol keys).

javascript

```
console.log(Reflect.ownKeys({ a: 1, [Symbol("b")]: 2 })); // ["a", Symbol(b)]
```

3. **Reflect in Proxies:**
   - Use Reflect to delegate default behavior in Proxy traps:

javascript

```
const target = { name: "Alice" };
const handler = {
  get(obj, prop) {
    console.log(`Accessing property: ${prop}`);
    return Reflect.get(obj, prop); // Default behavior
  },
};

const proxy = new Proxy(target, handler);
console.log(proxy.name); // Logs: "Accessing
property: name", Outputs: "Alice"
```

***Real-World Examples in Data Validation and Logging***

1. **Data Validation:**
   - Ensure object properties meet specific criteria:

     javascript

     ```
     const user = {};
     const handler = {
       set(obj, prop, value) {
     ```

```
    if (prop === "age" && (typeof value !== "number" || value <= 0)) {
      throw new Error("Age must be a positive number");
    }
    obj[prop] = value;
    return true;
  },
};

const proxy = new Proxy(user, handler);
proxy.age = 25; // Valid
proxy.age = -5; // Error: Age must be a positive number
```

2. **Logging Property Access:**
   - Log all property interactions for debugging:

javascript

```javascript
const target = { name: "Alice", age: 25 };
const handler = {
  get(obj, prop) {
    console.log(`Getting property: ${prop}`);
    return Reflect.get(obj, prop);
  },
```

```
  set(obj, prop, value) {
    console.log(`Setting property: ${prop} = ${value}`);
    return Reflect.set(obj, prop, value);
  },
};

const proxy = new Proxy(target, handler);
console.log(proxy.name); // Logs: "Getting property: name"
proxy.age = 30; // Logs: "Setting property: age = 30"
```

3. **Caching Function Calls:**
   - Use Proxies to implement function result caching:

javascript

```
function expensiveOperation(x) {
  console.log(`Calculating for ${x}`);
  return x * x;
}

const cache = new Map();
const handler = {
  apply(target, thisArg, args) {
```

```
    const key = args[0];
    if (cache.has(key)) {
      console.log(`Returning cached result for ${key}`);
      return cache.get(key);
    }
    const result = Reflect.apply(target, thisArg, args);
    cache.set(key, result);
    return result;
  },
};

const proxiedFunction = new Proxy(expensiveOperation, handler);

console.log(proxiedFunction(5)); // Logs: Calculating for 5, Outputs: 25
console.log(proxiedFunction(5)); // Logs: Returning cached result for 5, Outputs: 25
```

4. **Access Control:**
   - Restrict access to sensitive properties:

     javascript

```
const user = { name: "Alice", password: "secret" };
```

```
const handler = {
  get(obj, prop) {
    if (prop === "password") {
      throw new Error("Access denied");
    }
    return Reflect.get(obj, prop);
  },
};

const proxy = new Proxy(user, handler);
console.log(proxy.name); // "Alice"
console.log(proxy.password); // Error: Access
denied
```

***Best Practices for Proxies and Reflect***

1. **Use Proxies for Advanced Control:**
   - Proxies are ideal for logging, validation, and dynamic behavior. Use them when direct control over object operations is required.
2. **Delegate with Reflect for Clean Code:**
   - When implementing traps in Proxies, use Reflect to handle default operations to avoid duplicating logic.
3. **Avoid Overuse:**

    - Proxies add complexity. Use them judiciously and keep the handler logic simple.
4. **Combine Proxies with Data Structures:**
    - Pair Proxies with Map, Set, or WeakMap for caching, metadata, and advanced scenarios.

Proxies and the Reflect API provide unparalleled flexibility for controlling object interactions and enabling meta-programming. In the next chapter, we'll explore **Iterables and Async Iterables**, key concepts for working with sequential and asynchronous data in modern JavaScript. Let's dive in!

# CHAPTER 17: ES6 ITERABLES AND THE `for...of` LOOP

The concept of **iterables** was introduced in ES6, enabling JavaScript objects to define custom iteration behavior. This foundational feature powers constructs like the for...of loop, spread syntax, and destructuring. Iterables make it easy to process collections, streams, and sequences in a standardized way.

In this chapter, we'll explore what makes an object iterable, examine practical uses of for...of, and demonstrate how to combine iterables with other ES6 features.

### *What Makes an Object Iterable?*

1. **The Iterable Protocol:**
   - An object is considered iterable if it implements the Symbol.iterator method, which returns an iterator. The iterator is an object that adheres to the **iterator protocol**, providing a next() method that returns:
     - { value: <value>, done: false } when the iteration produces a value.
     - { value: undefined, done: true } when the iteration is complete.
2. **Built-in Iterables:**
   - Common iterable objects in JavaScript include:
     - **Arrays:** [1, 2, 3]
     - **Strings:** "hello"

        - **Maps:** new Map()
        - **Sets:** new Set()
    - These objects have a default Symbol.iterator method:

javascript

```
const arr = [1, 2, 3];
const iterator = arr[Symbol.iterator]();

console.log(iterator.next()); // { value: 1, done: false
}
console.log(iterator.next()); // { value: 2, done: false
}
console.log(iterator.next()); // { value: 3, done: false
}
console.log(iterator.next()); // { value: undefined,
done: true }
```

3. **Custom Iterables:**
    - You can make any object iterable by defining a Symbol.iterator method:

javascript

```
const customIterable = {
```

```
  data: [1, 2, 3],
  [Symbol.iterator]() {
   let index = 0;
   const { data } = this;

   return {
    next() {
     if (index < data.length) {
      return { value: data[index++], done: false };
     }
     return { value: undefined, done: true };
    },
   };
  },
};

for (const value of customIterable) {
  console.log(value); // 1, 2, 3
}
```

***Practical Uses of for...of in ES6***

The for...of loop simplifies iterating over iterable objects, such as arrays, strings, maps, and sets, compared to traditional for loops.

1. **Iterating Over Arrays:**

- Use for...of to iterate over array elements:

  ```javascript
  const fruits = ["apple", "banana", "cherry"];
  for (const fruit of fruits) {
    console.log(fruit);
  }
  ```

2. **Iterating Over Strings:**
   - Iterate over each character in a string:

     ```javascript
     const word = "hello";
     for (const char of word) {
       console.log(char); // h, e, l, l, o
     }
     ```

3. **Iterating Over Maps and Sets:**
   - **Maps:**
     - Use destructuring to access keys and values:

       ```javascript
       const map = new Map([
         ["name", "Alice"],
       ```

```
  ["age", 25],
]);

for (const [key, value] of map) {
  console.log(`${key}: ${value}`);
}
```

- **Sets:**
  - Iterate over unique values:

javascript

```javascript
const set = new Set([1, 2, 2, 3]);
for (const value of set) {
  console.log(value); // 1, 2, 3
}
```

4. **Combining with Spread Syntax:**
   - Use for...of for destructuring or combining iterables:

javascript

```javascript
const numbers = [1, 2, 3];
for (const num of [...numbers, 4, 5]) {
  console.log(num); // 1, 2, 3, 4, 5
}
```

5. **Iterating Over Arguments:**
   - Convert the arguments object into an iterable:

     javascript

     ```
     function logArguments(...args) {
       for (const arg of args) {
         console.log(arg);
       }
     }

     logArguments("hello", 42, true);
     ```

### *Combining Iterables with Other ES6 Features*

1. **Destructuring and Iterables:**
   - Destructure iterables directly:

     javascript

     ```
     const numbers = [1, 2, 3];
     const [first, ...rest] = numbers;
     console.log(first); // 1
     console.log(rest); // [2, 3]
     ```

2. **Generators and Iterables:**

- Generators simplify creating custom iterables:

```javascript
function* numberGenerator() {
  yield 1;
  yield 2;
  yield 3;
}

for (const num of numberGenerator()) {
  console.log(num); // 1, 2, 3
}
```

3. **Combining Iterables with Promise.all:**
   - Use iterables with asynchronous workflows:

```javascript
async function fetchData(ids) {
  const responses = await Promise.all(
    ids.map(id =>
fetch(`https://api.example.com/resource/${id}`))
  );
  for (const response of responses) {
    console.log(await response.json());
```

```
 }
}

fetchData([1, 2, 3]);
```

4. **Transforming Iterables:**
   - Use higher-order functions like map with iterables:

     javascript

     ```
     const numbers = [1, 2, 3];
     const doubled = [...numbers.map(num => num *
     2)];
     console.log(doubled); // [2, 4, 6]
     ```

5. **Creating Infinite Iterables:**
   - Combine generators with for...of for lazy evaluation:

     javascript

     ```
     function* infiniteSequence(start = 0) {
      let i = start;
      while (true) {
       yield i++;
      }
     }
     ```

```
const sequence = infiniteSequence();
for (const num of sequence) {
  if (num > 5) break;
  console.log(num); // 0, 1, 2, 3, 4, 5
}
```

### *Best Practices for Iterables and for...of*

1. **Use for...of for Clean Iteration:**
   - Prefer for...of over traditional loops for readability and flexibility when working with iterables.
2. **Combine Iterables with Generators:**
   - Use generators to create custom or infinite iterables efficiently.
3. **Pair Iterables with Destructuring:**
   - Leverage destructuring for cleaner code when extracting values.
4. **Validate Iterables:**
   - Ensure custom objects implement Symbol.iterator properly to avoid runtime errors in for...of loops.
5. **Optimize Performance with Lazy Iteration:**
   - Use generators or custom iterables for large datasets or sequences to avoid memory overhead.

Iterables and the for...of loop enhance JavaScript's ability to process sequential data. In the next chapter, we'll explore **JavaScript ES6 Classes in Depth**, focusing on object-oriented programming features like inheritance, encapsulation, and practical examples for real-world applications. Let's dive

# CHAPTER 18: NEW ARRAY METHODS IN ES6

ES6 and later updates introduced several new methods to enhance array manipulation, making JavaScript more expressive and efficient for tasks like searching, filtering, and iterating over data. These methods simplify common operations, improve readability, and reduce boilerplate code.

In this chapter, we'll explore new array methods such as find, findIndex, includes, and more. We'll also examine practical examples of filtering and searching data, and demonstrate how to combine these methods for powerful and efficient array manipulation.

## *Overview of New Array Methods*

1. **find:**
    - Returns the first element in an array that satisfies a provided testing function.
    - If no element satisfies the function, it returns undefined.

    javascript

```
const numbers = [5, 12, 8, 130, 44];
const found = numbers.find(num => num > 10);
console.log(found); // 12
```

2. **findIndex:**
   - Returns the index of the first element that satisfies a testing function.
   - Returns -1 if no element satisfies the function.

javascript

```
const numbers = [5, 12, 8, 130, 44];
const index = numbers.findIndex(num => num > 10);
console.log(index); // 1
```

3. **includes:**
   - Determines whether an array contains a specific value.
   - Returns true if the value is found, otherwise false.

javascript

```
const fruits = ["apple", "banana", "cherry"];
console.log(fruits.includes("banana")); // true
console.log(fruits.includes("orange")); // false
```

4. **some:**
   - Checks if at least one element satisfies a condition.
   - Returns true if the condition is met for any element, otherwise false.

   javascript

   ```
   const numbers = [1, 2, 3, 4, 5];
   console.log(numbers.some(num => num > 4)); //
   true
   console.log(numbers.some(num => num > 10)); //
   false
   ```

5. **every:**
   - Checks if all elements satisfy a condition.
   - Returns true if all elements meet the condition, otherwise false.

   javascript

   ```
   const numbers = [1, 2, 3, 4, 5];
   console.log(numbers.every(num => num > 0)); //
   true
   console.log(numbers.every(num => num > 3)); //
   false
   ```

6. **flat:**

- Flattens nested arrays to a specified depth.

  javascript

  ```
  const nested = [1, [2, [3, [4]]]];
  console.log(nested.flat(2)); // [1, 2, 3, [4]]
  ```

7. **flatMap:**
   - Maps each element using a mapping function, then flattens the result by one level.

     javascript

     ```
     const words = ["hello", "world"];
     console.log(words.flatMap(word => word.split(""))); // ["h", "e", "l", "l", "o", "w", "o", "r", "l", "d"]
     ```

***Practical Examples in Filtering and Searching Data***

1. **Finding Specific Objects in an Array:**
   - Use find to locate an object with specific properties.

     javascript

     ```
     const users = [
     ```

```
  { id: 1, name: "Alice" },
  { id: 2, name: "Bob" },
  { id: 3, name: "Charlie" },
];

const user = users.find(user => user.id === 2);
console.log(user); // { id: 2, name: "Bob" }
```

2. **Checking Existence with includes:**
   - Use includes to verify if a value is present in an array.

     javascript

     ```
     const roles = ["admin", "editor", "viewer"];
     console.log(roles.includes("admin")); // true
     console.log(roles.includes("guest")); // false
     ```

3. **Filtering Arrays with some and every:**
   - Validate conditions across elements in an array.

     javascript

     ```
     const scores = [85, 92, 88, 75, 95];

     // Check if any score is below 80
     ```

```
console.log(scores.some(score => score < 80)); //
true

// Check if all scores are above 70
console.log(scores.every(score => score > 70)); //
true
```

4. **Flattening Nested Arrays with flat:**
   - Simplify nested structures for easier processing.

     javascript

     ```
     const nested = [1, [2, [3, [4]]]];
     const flattened = nested.flat(2);
     console.log(flattened); // [1, 2, 3, [4]]
     ```

5. **Transforming and Flattening with flatMap:**
   - Simplify complex transformations in one step.

     javascript

     ```
     const transactions = ["+100", "-50", "+75"];
     const numbers = transactions.flatMap(trans =>
     parseInt(trans));
     console.log(numbers); // [100, -50, 75]
     ```

***Combining New Methods for Efficient Array Manipulation***

1. **Chaining Methods:**
   - Combine multiple array methods for streamlined operations.

     javascript

     ```
     const products = [
       { id: 1, name: "Laptop", price: 1000 },
       { id: 2, name: "Phone", price: 500 },
       { id: 3, name: "Tablet", price: 300 },
     ];

     const affordableProducts = products
       .filter(product => product.price < 800)
       .map(product => product.name);

     console.log(affordableProducts); // ["Phone",
     "Tablet"]
     ```

2. **Deduplication with includes:**
   - Remove duplicates by leveraging includes.

     javascript

     ```
     const array = [1, 2, 2, 3, 4, 4, 5];
     ```

```
const unique = array.filter((item, index) =>
!array.slice(0, index).includes(item));
console.log(unique); // [1, 2, 3, 4, 5]
```

3. **Complex Filtering:**
   - Combine findIndex and splice to find and remove items.

     javascript

```
const tasks = [
  { id: 1, task: "Do laundry" },
  { id: 2, task: "Write report" },
  { id: 3, task: "Prepare dinner" },
];

const index = tasks.findIndex(task => task.id ===
2);
if (index !== -1) {
  tasks.splice(index, 1);
}
console.log(tasks); // [{ id: 1, task: "Do laundry" },
{ id: 3, task: "Prepare dinner" }]
```

4. **Nested Data Transformation:**
   - Use flatMap to simplify nested transformations.

```javascript
const users = [
  { id: 1, activities: ["login", "viewed products"] },
  { id: 2, activities: ["logout", "purchased"] },
];

const allActivities = users.flatMap(user => user.activities);
console.log(allActivities); // ["login", "viewed products", "logout", "purchased"]
```

### *Best Practices for Using New Array Methods*

1. **Understand Method Purpose:**
   - Use find and findIndex for locating single elements, and filter for multiple matches.
   - Use includes for simple existence checks.
2. **Combine Methods for Efficiency:**
   - Chain methods like filter and map to reduce iteration overhead and improve readability.
3. **Optimize Performance:**
   - Avoid chaining unnecessarily when a single method suffices. For example, prefer find over filter if only one match is needed.

4. **Use flat and flatMap for Nested Data:**
   - Simplify complex operations by leveraging these methods for transforming and flattening.
5. **Validate Edge Cases:**
   - Ensure that methods like find handle cases where no match is found (returning undefined).

With these new array methods, JavaScript provides robust tools for efficient and readable data manipulation. In the next chapter, we'll explore **Promises in Depth**, focusing on advanced patterns like chaining, error handling, and real-world asynchronous workflows. Let's continue!

# CHAPTER 19: ES6 IN PRACTICE – BUILDING REAL-WORLD APPLICATIONS

The ES6 features we've explored are not just theoretical improvements—they are designed to make JavaScript development scalable, maintainable, and efficient. By integrating these tools and concepts into real-world applications, developers can write cleaner, more modular, and easier-to-understand code.

In this chapter, we'll build a sample project that demonstrates ES6 in action, focus on leveraging ES6 features for scalability and maintainability, and examine common patterns and best practices in modern development.

### *Putting It All Together with a Sample Project*

We'll build a **Task Management Application** using ES6 features, including classes, modules, destructuring, promises, and more.

**Project: Task Management Application**

**Features:**

- Add, edit, delete, and list tasks.
- Save tasks to a mock API using Promises.
- Use ES6 features for cleaner and modular code.

**Step 1: Project Structure**

Organize the project with modular files:

bash

```
src/
├── app.js         # Entry point
├── taskManager.js # Task management logic
└── api.js         # Mock API logic
```

**Step 2: Mock API Logic**

Create a src/api.js module to simulate API interactions:

javascript

```
// src/api.js
export const mockAPI = (() => {
  const database = [];
```

```
  return {
    getTasks() {
      return new Promise(resolve => setTimeout(() =>
resolve([...database]), 500));
    },
    addTask(task) {
      return new Promise(resolve => {
        database.push(task);
        setTimeout(() => resolve(task), 500);
      });
    },
    deleteTask(id) {
      return new Promise(resolve => {
        const index = database.findIndex(task => task.id === id);
        if (index !== -1) {
          const removed = database.splice(index, 1);
          setTimeout(() => resolve(removed[0]), 500);
        } else {
          setTimeout(() => resolve(null), 500);
        }
      });
    },
  };
})();
```

**Step 3: Task Management Logic**

Create a src/taskManager.js module for managing tasks:

javascript

```
// src/taskManager.js
import { mockAPI } from "./api.js";

export class TaskManager {
  constructor() {
    this.tasks = [];
  }

  async loadTasks() {
    this.tasks = await mockAPI.getTasks();
    console.log("Tasks loaded:", this.tasks);
  }

  async addTask(title, description) {
    const newTask = {
      id: Date.now(),
      title,
      description,
      createdAt: new Date(),
```

```
    };
    const savedTask = await mockAPI.addTask(newTask);
    this.tasks.push(savedTask);
    console.log("Task added:", savedTask);
  }

  async deleteTask(id) {
    const removedTask = await mockAPI.deleteTask(id);
    if (removedTask) {
      this.tasks = this.tasks.filter(task => task.id !== id);
      console.log("Task deleted:", removedTask);
    } else {
      console.log(`Task with ID ${id} not found.`);
    }
  }

  listTasks() {
    console.log("Current Tasks:");
    this.tasks.forEach(({ id, title, description }) => {
      console.log(`- [${id}] ${title}: ${description}`);
    });
  }
}
```

**Step 4: Application Entry Point**

Use src/app.js to interact with the TaskManager:

javascript

```
// src/app.js
import { TaskManager } from "./taskManager.js";

(async function main() {
  const manager = new TaskManager();

  // Load initial tasks
  await manager.loadTasks();

  // Add a task
  await manager.addTask("Learn ES6", "Practice JavaScript ES6 features");
  await manager.addTask("Build Project", "Use ES6 to create a task manager app");

  // List tasks
  manager.listTasks();

  // Delete a task
  const [firstTask] = manager.tasks;
  if (firstTask) {
    await manager.deleteTask(firstTask.id);
```

```
    manager.listTasks();
  }
})();
```

### *Using ES6 Features to Build Scalable, Maintainable Code*

1. **Modules for Separation of Concerns:**
   - Use ES6 modules (import and export) to separate logic into focused, reusable files.
   - Example: taskManager.js handles task operations, while api.js handles mock API logic.
2. **Classes for Encapsulation:**
   - Use ES6 classes to encapsulate related functionality and maintain state.
   - Example: The TaskManager class manages tasks with methods for CRUD operations.
3. **Promises and Async/Await for Asynchronous Operations:**
   - Simplify API calls with async/await instead of nested callbacks.
   - Example: The addTask and deleteTask methods in TaskManager use await for cleaner asynchronous workflows.
4. **Destructuring for Readability:**

   - Extract specific properties from objects and arrays for cleaner code.
   - Example: Destructure id, title, and description in listTasks.
5. **Template Literals for Dynamic Strings:**
   - Use template literals to create dynamic, readable output.
   - Example: Log task details in listTasks using template strings.

### *Common Patterns and Best Practices in Modern Development*

1. **Separation of Concerns:**
   - Keep distinct responsibilities in separate modules to improve maintainability and reusability.
2. **Leverage Iterables and for...of:**
   - Use for...of to iterate over tasks instead of manually managing loop counters.
3. **Use Arrow Functions for Simplicity:**
   - Prefer arrow functions for concise and lexical this in callbacks.
4. **Handle Errors Gracefully:**
   - Wrap asynchronous logic in try-catch blocks to handle potential errors.

```javascript
try {
  await manager.addTask("Invalid Task");
} catch (error) {
  console.error("Error adding task:", error);
}
```

5. **Optimize Performance with Spread and Rest:**
   - Use the spread operator to clone or merge arrays and objects efficiently.
6. **Consistent Coding Style:**
   - Adhere to a consistent code style for readability and collaboration. Use linters like ESLint to enforce standards.

By combining ES6 features, we can build modular, readable, and maintainable JavaScript applications. The Task Management Application showcases how classes, modules, promises, and other ES6 tools streamline real-world development.

In the next chapter, we'll discuss **Tooling and Debugging ES6 Code**, focusing on tools, linters, and debuggers that enhance the development experience for modern JavaScript applications. Let's continue!

# CHAPTER 20: LOOKING AHEAD – BEYOND ES6

The introduction of ES6 revolutionized JavaScript, providing features that improved readability, scalability, and performance. However, JavaScript has continued to evolve, with newer ECMAScript versions adding even more capabilities. In this chapter, we'll explore how ES6 compatibility is handled with tools like Babel, provide an overview of key features introduced post-ES6, and discuss future trends in JavaScript development.

## *ES6 Compatibility and Transpilation with Babel*

While ES6 brought powerful enhancements, its adoption faced compatibility issues with older browsers and environments that lacked support for the new syntax and features. Transpilation emerged as a solution to bridge this gap.

1. **What is Babel?**
   - Babel is a JavaScript compiler that translates modern JavaScript (ES6 and beyond) into an older version (usually ES5) compatible with older browsers.

- It enables developers to use the latest JavaScript features without worrying about compatibility.

2. **Setting Up Babel:**
   - Install Babel using npm:

     bash

     ```
     npm install --save-dev @babel/core @babel/cli @babel/preset-env
     ```

   - Create a Babel configuration file (.babelrc):

     json

     ```
     {
       "presets": ["@babel/preset-env"]
     }
     ```

   - Transpile files:

     bash

     ```
     npx babel src --out-dir dist
     ```

3. **Using Babel with Webpack:**
   - Babel integrates seamlessly with build tools like Webpack for automated transpilation:

```javascript
// webpack.config.js
module.exports = {
  module: {
    rules: [
      {
        test: /\.js$/,
        exclude: /node_modules/,
        use: {
          loader: "babel-loader",
        },
      },
    ],
  },
};
```

4. **Targeting Specific Browsers:**
   - Use @babel/preset-env to define browser compatibility targets:

```json
{
  "presets": [
    [
```

```
        "@babel/preset-env",
        {
          "targets": "> 0.25%, not dead"
        }
      ]
    ]
  }
```

### *Overview of Newer JavaScript Features Post-ES6*

The ECMAScript standard continues to evolve yearly, introducing new features and improvements. Here are key highlights from versions post-ES6:

1. **ES2017 (ES8):**
    - **async/await:** Simplifies working with Promises for asynchronous operations.

      ```javascript
      async function fetchData() {
        const response = await fetch("https://api.example.com/data");
        return response.json();
      }
      ```

- **Object.entries() and Object.values():** Iterate over object keys/values.

javascript

```
const obj = { a: 1, b: 2 };
console.log(Object.entries(obj)); // [["a", 1], ["b",
2]]
console.log(Object.values(obj)); // [1, 2]
```

2. **ES2018 (ES9):**
   - **Rest/Spread for Objects:**

javascript

```
const obj = { a: 1, b: 2, c: 3 };
const { a, ...rest } = obj;
console.log(rest); // { b: 2, c: 3 }
```

   - **Promise.finally():**
     - Execute code after a Promise is settled (fulfilled or rejected).

javascript

```
fetch("https://api.example.com/data")
  .then(data => console.log(data))
```

```
.catch(err => console.error(err))
.finally(() => console.log("Operation
completed"));
```

3. **ES2019 (ES10):**
   - **Array.flat() and Array.flatMap():**

     ```javascript
     const nested = [1, [2, [3]]];
     console.log(nested.flat(2)); // [1, 2, 3]
     ```

   - **Object.fromEntries():**
     - Converts an array of key-value pairs into an object.

       ```javascript
       const entries = [["a", 1], ["b", 2]];
       console.log(Object.fromEntries(entries)); //
       { a: 1, b: 2 }
       ```

4. **ES2020:**
   - **Nullish Coalescing Operator (??):**
     - Returns the right-hand operand if the left-hand operand is null or undefined.

```javascript
const value = null ?? "default";
console.log(value); // "default"
```

- **Optional Chaining (?.):**
  - Simplifies accessing deeply nested properties.

```javascript
const user = { profile: { name: "Alice" } };
console.log(user?.profile?.name); // "Alice"
console.log(user?.settings?.theme); // undefined
```

5. **ES2021 and Beyond:**
   - **Logical Assignment Operators:**

```javascript
let a = null;
a ??= "default";
console.log(a); // "default"
```

   - **String.replaceAll():**

javascript

```
const text = "hello world, world";
console.log(text.replaceAll("world", "JavaScript"));
// "hello JavaScript, JavaScript"
```

- **Top-Level await:**
  - Use await at the top level of modules:

    javascript

    ```
    const data = await
    fetch("https://api.example.com/data").then(r
    es => res.json());
    console.log(data);
    ```

### *Future Trends in JavaScript Development*

1. **Increased Focus on Tooling and Ecosystem:**
   - **TypeScript:** Strongly typed JavaScript is becoming more common for reducing runtime errors and improving IDE support.
   - **ESLint/Prettier:** Linters and formatters are now essential for maintaining code quality and consistency.

   - **Vite:** Tools like Vite are replacing older build systems for faster development workflows.
2. **Server-Side JavaScript:**
   - JavaScript continues to dominate on the server with frameworks like Next.js (for React) and Deno, offering modern features like built-in TypeScript support.
3. **Functional Programming Paradigms:**
   - Modern JavaScript heavily borrows from functional programming, emphasizing immutability, higher-order functions, and lazy evaluation.
4. **Edge Computing and Serverless:**
   - JavaScript is pivotal in edge computing environments like Cloudflare Workers or AWS Lambda, where small, modular scripts are deployed near users for low-latency applications.
5. **JavaScript in New Domains:**
   - **WebAssembly (Wasm):** JavaScript integrates with WebAssembly for performance-intensive tasks.
   - **IoT and Robotics:** Frameworks like Johnny-Five and libraries like Web Bluetooth extend JavaScript into hardware programming.
6. **Standardization and Simplification:**

- Proposals like **Temporal API** (for date/time handling) aim to address long-standing gaps in JavaScript.

### *Best Practices for Future-Proof Development*

1. **Adopt Transpilation Early:**
    - Use Babel or similar tools to ensure compatibility with older environments while adopting modern syntax.
2. **Stay Updated on New Standards:**
    - Regularly review ECMAScript updates to incorporate new features.
3. **Write Modular, Maintainable Code:**
    - Emphasize modularity and maintainability to ease future upgrades.
4. **Embrace Type Safety:**
    - Adopt TypeScript or JSDoc annotations for better tooling and error prevention.
5. **Experiment with New Tools:**
    - Stay flexible by experimenting with emerging frameworks and tools.

JavaScript continues to evolve, solidifying its position as one of the most versatile programming languages. By staying updated with new features and trends, developers can leverage JavaScript for both current and future challenges. Whether building web applications, server-side systems, or even IoT devices, ES6 and beyond provide the foundation for robust, scalable solutions.

This chapter concludes our exploration of ES6 and modern JavaScript. Continue building on this knowledge to master advanced concepts and create cutting-edge applications. Happy coding!

www.ingramcontent.com/pod-product-compliance
Lightning Source LLC
LaVergne TN
LVHW051328050326
832903LV00031B/3421

* 9 7 9 8 3 0 0 5 5 9 8 0 9 *